Trading E-mini Stock Index Futures

Trading E-mini Stock Index Futures

A New Path to Wealth

Dennis B. Anderson, Ed.D.

TRADING E-MINI STOCK INDEX FUTURES
A NEW PATH TO WEALTH

iUniverse books may be ordered through booksellers or by contacting:

iUniverse
1663 Liberty Drive
Bloomington, IN 47403
www.iuniverse.com
1-800-Authors (1-800-288-4677)

ISBN: 978-1-5320-0869-6 (sc)
ISBN: 978-1-5320-0870-2 (hc)
ISBN: 978-1-5320-0868-9 (e)

Library of Congress Control Number: 2016916776

Print information available on the last page.

iUniverse rev. date: 01/13/2017

Limit of Liability/Disclaimer of Warranty

Contents

This book is dedicated to my grandsons,
Justin and Carson

Abbreviations

AAII	American Association of Individual Investors
CBOE	Chicago Board Options Exchange
CCI	Consumer Confidence Index
CME	Chicago Mercantile Exchange
CPI	Consumer Price Index
DOW	Dow Jones Industrial average of thirty large company stocks
ECB	European Central Bank
EMA	Exponential Moving Average
EMD	E-mini Standard and Poor's (S & P) Midcap 400 Stock Index
E-mini	An electronically traded stock index futures contract
ES	E-mini Standard and Poor's (S & P) 500 Stock Index
ETF	Exchange Traded Fund
FOMC	Federal Open Market Committee
GDP	Gross Domestic Product
GTC	Good Till Cancelled order
LEAPS	Long Term Equity Anticipation Security Options

MACD	Moving Average Convergence Divergence indicator
9X	Nine-period exponential moving average indicator
NQ	E-mini NASDAQ 100 Stock Index
PMI	Purchasing Managers Index
PPI	Producer Price Index
RSI	Relative Strength Index indicator
SMA	Simple Moving Average
TF	E-mini Russell 2000 Small Cap Index
3X	Three-period exponential moving average indicator
VIX	Chicago Board Options Exchange Volatility Index
YM	E-mini DOW 30 Stock Index

Preface

Rule Number One: Never lose money.
Rule Number Two: Never forget Rule Number One - - Warren Buffett

Do you believe in the inherent upward bias of the U. S. stock market? Are you willing to allocate about five percent to ten percent of your portfolio for trading, with the prospect of earning up to 150% or more per year trading this amount? Do you have the desire and ability to understand how the market works, the maturity to administer an investment plan, and the patience and self-discipline to manage your own emotions and behaviors? If so, this book is for you.

This book is for those of you who are dissatisfied and frustrated with your investment outcomes, have accumulated some capital, and are looking for ways to take personal control over at least part of your finances. I have been where you are.

My early life was spent on a farm in northeastern Nebraska, near the small Swedish community of Wausa. I was fortunate to have a large, loving family, but we were never able to have more than the basic necessities of life, no matter how hard we worked. I knew I had to go to college and achieve a good education, because I never wanted to be poor as an adult.

After a bachelor's degree, two years as a public school teacher, then a master's and doctorate in psychology from the University of Nebraska at Lincoln, I accepted a professorial faculty position at Southern Illinois University. Professional focus was on clinical, criminal and forensic psychology. This included studies and research in probability theory, and the history, pathology, and issues involved in all types of gambling. I consulted regularly, conducted thousands of clinical evaluations, and managed twelve grant projects, along with teaching and the usual university responsibilities. I also provided years of service as a forensic medical expert for the Social Security Administration's Court of Appeals. I retired at the age of 58 after thirty years of essentially working three jobs.

Early on, I went to a broker, and she recommended a great growth stock opportunity. Six months later, the company went belly up. Fortunately, my losses were not great. I know there are many good brokers available to help, and people who need them, but I knew I could learn to invest with at least this level of success. So, at about the age of thirty, I began my quest to learn all I could about economics, taxes, the influences of politics, and the many issues and avenues related to investing. Since then, I have always completed my own taxes, managed every dollar of my investments, and have been very successful.

As a part-time trader, using the models I created, I have earned over $400,000 the past three years. I now want to share what I have learned, so you too may profit.

The impetus for this book began as I pondered the question, "What is the legacy we want to leave for our children and grandchildren." We naturally think of notions such as honesty, the values of a good education and hard work, pride in ourselves and the products of our efforts, and a spiritual foundation.

As I thought over my efforts, and how I achieved financial success, I wondered how I could share some of these values and lessons. I'm reminded of the expression, "Give a man a fish, and he eats for a day. Teach a man to fish, and he will eat for a lifetime."

I have two wonderful grandsons who are in middle school. I want to leave some resources to help secure their financial future, and I thought of a variation to the above thoughts. "Give your heirs some money, and that will add to their resources until it is gone. Teach them how to earn additional money, and they can supplement their income for a lifetime, and perhaps the lifetime of their children."

So, I began thinking how I could prepare a guide for them so they could learn how to successfully trade e-mini stock index futures. I had created and developed so much information, I couldn't boil it down to a usable summary for them. One day, I was discussing this dilemma with Dr. Jeanne Peters (also a psychologist), the wonderful woman in my life, and she said, "Have you ever thought about writing a book?" And so it began.

Acknowledgements

Special thanks to Jeanne Peters, who encouraged and supported me through the process of organizing and writing this book. My thanks to my daughter, Erika, for her technical expertise and advice. Appreciation is given to Suzanne Lee, from ImageWurks, for her production of the candlestick images and charts. And, thanks is given to the staff at iUniverse for their support in the publication of this book.

Chapter 1

Introduction

A stock index e-mini is an electronically traded futures contract that represents an agreement to buy or sell the cash value of the underlying index at a date specified by its expiration. Values of the stock index e-minis vary, and contracts are sized at their individual value multiplied by the futures price. Because the indexes trade on a multiple of the cash value of the stock index each represents, they are settled in cash. This makes them an attractive trading vehicle for individual investors.

E-minis were first developed in 1997 with the introduction of the e-mini S&P 500. It trades at one-fifth the size of the full-sized contract, making it more accessible to smaller investors. Other e-mini stock index futures were added later with similar proportional relationships to their indexes.

Individual stocks have vulnerabilities concerning management, the economy, competition, and other exogenous factors that might affect their prices. Trading costs also weigh against profits. In comparison, e-mini stock index futures consist of hundreds of companies;

therefore, risk and volatility are balanced. Leverage greatly increases profits, even when trading only one contract, and my models restrict possible losses. Trading fees are only about seven dollars for a round-trip trade of one contract.

These are the e-mini stock index futures you will learn about and trade. The ES (trade symbol /ES) has the same composition as the S & P 500 Index, representing 500 of the largest corporations in the United States. The NQ (trade symbol/NQ) represents the NASDAQ 100 index. The YM (trade symbol/YM), represents the DOW 30 Stock Index. The EMD (trade symbol/EMD) represents the S & P Midcap 400 Stock Index. And the TF (trade symbol/TF) represents the Russell 2000 Small Cap Index.

These e-mini stock index futures are largely ignored in the areas of investing/trading, and you rarely find any meaningful discussion, analysis, or methods for trading in this area. We will fill that deficit in the pages ahead.

Readers of this book will vary considerably in age, experience, and levels of understanding concerning the material contained herein. Since all readers need to proceed from the same levels of understanding, chapter two will describe the history of stock market investing, and the various options that have been developed.

Chapter three provides necessary information regarding technical indicators and reports. These are used by other traders to make decisions, and you need to understand them and how they influence stock market futures. Over twenty regular government-related reports and influences are included. These are seldom discussed, but are extremely important in preparing for short-term movements in the markets.

Psychological issues are explained in Chapter 4. Cognitive and emotional thinking are described. You will learn more about yourself, your emotions, and how to use greater insight in making trading decisions.

In Chapter 5 you will learn about e-mini stock index futures and how to trade them. This is a vital foundation for successful trading.

Candlestick definitions and reversal formations are instrumental in understanding price movements and price reversals. The information in Chapter 6 explains how to interpret and incorporate candlestick analysis into your trading success.

The first trading model, Follow the Money, is described in Chapter 7. I will show you how to set up this model, and how to successfully manage trades for consistent profits. I will also explain how to minimize risk.

Chapter 8 explains Model 2, Enjoy Those "Index Bites." You will learn more about reading market action as it relates to making profits, and I will explain how to set up this model for trading. This is an active and fun way to trade on a part-time basis, and will provide steady regular profits that will produce monthly income of several thousand dollars.

Model 3, Buy Low, Sell High; Buy Lower, Sell Higher, is explained in Chapter 9. This is the most passive model, but it produces great profits when the market suffers a decline in price. Levels and procedures are described for buying at specific price decline percentages. When the market recovers, you bank your profits.

Chapter 10 includes a review of important points to remember as well as new final information to help you on your "new path to wealth."

A glossary of important terms follows Chapter 10. I have alphabetically defined and explained terms as they appear in the text. If you want to refresh your understanding, please consult the glossary.

As a professor, I always wanted my students to learn and understand the information I gave them. And, since they were going to apply this information in the real world, I wanted them to understand themselves and how they were interpreting what I was teaching them.

I emphasized what information was most important, and told them everything that was going to be on each test. Those who stayed focused and serious, and worked to understand and apply what I was teaching were very successful.

My goal in writing this book is for all of you to be successful traders in this e-mini area. For that to happen, you need to carefully read, and take the time to understand, everything that is in this book. The pages are not many, but all the material is very important and relevant. The chapters are additive, so it is also necessary for you to read everything in the order presented. It will not be productive to jump around. Take time to digest and practice what you are about to read.

Chapter 2

History of Stock Investing

Choose a job you love, and you will never have to work a day in your life. - - Confucious

We're all familiar with the stock market crash of 1929. That prompted regulations regarding how commercial markets were managed. Stock markets survived major wars and economic gyrations into the 1970's. This decade began the real expansion of market opportunities for the individual investor.

A stock mutual fund is a combination of many stocks, supposedly with a common theme such as company size, value or growth stocks, blend of types, international stocks, and more recently sector and other specialized funds.

John Bogle is credited with the formation of Vanguard, a mutual fund company that is essentially owned by the shareholders. Bogle introduced the index fund in the 1970's. Managers of these index funds simply buy the stocks of an existing index, such as the S & P 500. The advantage of such a fund is lower fees, since researchers are not needed to select stocks. Index funds stay fully invested, so they perform well in up markets, but will fall further in down markets.

Managed mutual funds are buying and selling stocks, usually more frequently than index funds, and need a cash reserve to cover anticipated redemptions. Therefore, they often fare better in a down market. But, since they have cash reserves, and higher expenses due to research and management, they usually perform less well than index funds in an advancing market. Bogle has said, in effect, that you might as well just buy the market (index fund), since it is extremely difficult to beat the market through managed funds because of the higher expenses.

Exchange Traded Fund

An Exchange Traded Fund (ETF) came about after the creation of mutual funds. Exchange Traded Funds contain a collection of stocks or bonds, like mutual funds, but they have more specific characteristics and focus, and their costs are usually lower than those of a mutual fund. An ETF can be bought and sold any time the market is open, the same as a stock. Mutual funds, on the other hand, are sold only at the end of the day, and at the closing price for that day. That means when you sell a mutual fund, you do not know what the closing price will be at the time of your sale. The advantage of an ETF is that you can indicate what price you will accept to buy or sell, and you are usually able to get that price. ETF's have expanded greatly, and there are now over 1700 different ETF's. Not all of them are a good investment, however, and you need to tread carefully before you invest.

Stock Options

A stock option is a contract to buy or sell a stock or some other equity product such as an ETF. It has a specific price (strike price), and an expiration date. If an option expires, it ceases to have any value, and no longer exists. There are two basic types of options, puts and calls, and you can sell or buy either type.

Options are complex, and not for a novice investor. Large investment firms, and traders, move the markets through large option positions. The newer, and smaller, player can get pulled under by getting into this market. Here are some of the terms used to describe how you might trade options: buy to open, sell to open, buy to close, sell to close, write puts (go short), write calls (go long), bear call spread, bear put spread, option call spread, LEAPS, straddles, strangles, and iron condor. These terms indicate the complexities of trading options.

Volatility Index

The Chicago Board Options Exchange (CBOE) Volatility Index (VIX) measures volatility of the S & P 500 by analyzing option positions placed by traders. This index measures fear in the stock market, as more traders trade options for protection when uncertainty stresses the market. When the S & P has a substantial decline, the VIX rises sharply. When the S & P is calm, or mildly ascending, the VIX will be lower. A VIX of 10-20 corresponds to a calm, often complacent market attitude. A range of 20-30 suggests uncertainty and nervousness among investors. Scores above thirty correspond to large amounts of volatility as a result of elevated feelings of fear on the part of investors. They have reasons to be concerned about the predictability of future market directions. The VIX can also be traded, but you can find better trades in other areas.

Penny Stocks

As the name implies, these are usually stocks priced less than a dollar. In fact, many are priced in the range of five cents to 25 cents per share. You might be thinking, "Wow, this is a great opportunity to buy 10,000 shares at five cents ($500), then sell them for twenty cents apiece ($2,000). What a nifty way to quadruple my money." Not so fast.

These are unlisted small entities that hype themselves as the next great thing (think Apple or Netflix or Bitcoin). Fact is, most of them "die on the vine." If you receive a mailing, or email talking up one of these micro companies, run, don't walk away. Trash or delete. Sometimes, you receive a solicitation from someone claiming to be endorsing this company, and highly recommending you buy this stock.

Read the fine print. These people are being paid to try to get you to "invest." They have also "had the opportunity to get an 'advance investment' ahead of the public solicitation." This is called "Pump and Dump," one of the oldest cons in the game. Think about it.

Why are these people wanting naive investors to buy this stock? Since these offerings are very thinly traded, and there are limited numbers of shares, these stocks are extremely volatile, and their prices move quickly and strongly. If they can get enough gullible and greedy people to buy this stock, the price will quickly rise and the solicitor will be the first one out the door, once they think the run-up in price has reached its max. That leaves the rest of the buyers holding the bag, as the price quickly drops back to where it started, or lower. There are some who may have gambled on an exit strategy, and dumped their stock for more than they paid, but most will get out near the bottom, and accept their losses. Remember, these companies do not pay dividends and, for the most part, are not currently delivering goods or services. You are being asked to "invest for potential."

Hedge Funds

A hedge fund is an investment fund that pools money from high net worth individual investors, and uses complex, and often high-risk strategies in hopes of earning above-average returns. The hedge fund manager has a great deal of discretion, and may enter long and short positions in futures and options, and invest in areas including stocks, bonds, currencies, and commodities. They may also increase their leverage by using borrowed money. The success of such funds is mixed, and many have closed the past two years. Hedge funds lost an estimated $78 billion during August, 2015. Investors usually have fees of two percent per year on their invested assets, and the manager of the fund usually gets about twenty percent of all profits off the top. Typical minimum investment in a hedge fund is between $500,000 and $1,000,000.

Don't gamble; take all your savings and buy some good stock and hold it till it goes up, then sell it. If it don't go up, don't buy it. - - Will Rogers

Stock Market Axioms

Information in this section comes from the Stock Trader's Almanac, Ned Davis Research, Investopedia.com and other web sites, various publications, and several of the books I have read. As we know, history is not a predictor of the future; however, those who have studied stock markets over the years look for patterns that show consistency and relevancy, and may also show correlations with certain days, months, and years. (Correlations are not causal; they only show relationships.) If patterns emerge, we tend to view them as not only descriptive, but perhaps predictive due to their often routine presence.

We must, however, keep in mind the evolutionary nature of stock markets throughout the world. Much of this collected data is based on information from U.S. markets between 1950 and 2010. There have been many changes over the past two decades. We have witnessed the development of the internet; on-line trading; the use of computers, algorithms, and high-frequency trading by professionals; and instant world-wide information flow via the internet. These changes have begun to reduce the predictability of patterns from earlier decades. So, while the following axioms are interesting, and many have earlier patterns of consistency, the investment world continues to undergo changes that may make some of these less helpful in the future. All references to the market, or the stock market described in this section refer to the S & P 500 Stock Index (S & P), unless otherwise indicated.

Whenever researchers conduct independent long-term historical research, there are slight differences in their outcomes. This could be due to actual differences in length of time, time period included in the study, methodology, operational definitions, or possibly different indexes. As I researched the history of the stock market, I chose numbers that were closest to consensus.

A Bull Market describes a period of steadily rising stock prices. A Bear Market describes a period of steadily falling stock prices. In each case, prices may temporarily change direction, but the trend remains.

A stock market correction is a reverse movement, usually negative, in a stock, bond, commodity, or index. This usually describes a price decline that interrupts an uptrend in prices. Professional traders and money managers often reserve the term of a correction to a drop of at least ten percent in price.

The average Bull Market lasts three years, with an average (mean) appreciation of 81%. The average Bear Market lasts eight months, with an average loss of -31%. From 1982 to 2000 there was a Bull Market; 2000 to 2002, a Bear Market; 2002 to 2007, a Bull Market; 2007 to 2008, a Bear Market; and 2008 to 2014, a Bull Market.

There are 252 trading days each year. There is a five percent correction every fifty trading days, on average; about five per year. There is a 10% correction every 161 trading days; about three every two years. A correction of 20% or more occurs about every 635 trading days, or one about every two and a half years. When the S & P has dropped at least five percent, the mean drop is 8.2%. When the S & P has dropped at least 10%, the mean drop is 12%.

Toward the end of a bull market, there are technical divergences. This usually means large-capitalization stocks move higher, but small-cap stocks lag, and stock leadership narrows. At the beginning of a bull market, small-cap stocks usually move higher earlier and faster than large-caps.

The stock market has had rising prices every thirty-day period before a national election. During the third year of a presidential cycle, the S & P 500 Index and the DOW have risen an average of 16%. Years ending in five have had only two down years in the past thirteen decades (2015 being the second year). Before 2015, average gain in these "five" numbered years was 28% for the DOW, and 25% for the S & P.

In the past 84 years, there have only been four times when equity markets were up double digits three years in a row, 2012 to 2014 being the last. In each of these occurrences, the fourth year was up an average of 23%, not counting 2015.

When the American Association of Individual Investors (AAII) Bulls and Bears Survey drops to a very low ratio of many more bears than bulls, that has typically been a bullish contrarian indicator that has preceded an average gain of 7.7% in the S & P six months after such readings, according to Jack Albin, Chief Investment Officer of BMO Bank.

It is estimated that about 70% to 80% of total stock market volume is now driven by computer-managed algorithmic traders. As prices move lower, sell programs are triggered, setting off a cascade of further sell programs, driving the market lower. This exacerbates the market's reaction to negative news.

The period of late July to early October is the worst time for stocks. Since 1950, the ten-week period between July 17 and September 25 has produced an average return of -2.0%. This equates to more than twelve years of data. August and September is the worst consecutive two-month period.

You're probably familiar with the phrase, "Sell in May and walk away." Early May, to the end of October, is the worst consecutive six-month period for stocks. Technically, you come out ahead if you're in the market November through April, then convert to cash and/or bonds the next six months. This is not practical, however, as you have transaction costs and tax considerations. Also, this doesn't turn out positively every year, and February is often a break even or down month.

December is the best singular month for stocks, gaining an average 1.7% over the period of 1950-2014. The best three-month period is November-January, averaging 4.2%. The "Santa Claus rally" includes Christmas shopping, and end-of-year spending, but specifically focuses on the last five trading days of the year, and the first two trading days of January. Average gain over these seven days is 1.5% since 1980.

Losing stocks are often sold the first two weeks of December, so investors can claim these capital losses against their income for tax deductions. These beaten down stocks tend to outperform the following two months from mid December to mid February.

This also applies to small companies, and the "January effect." Small cap stocks are volatile, and investors often have losses they wish to use as deductions from their income. So, they sell small stocks in December, then they, or other investors buy them in January of the following year. If you engage in this practice, be cognizant of the "thirty-day wash rule" which states you may not buy back the same stock, or equity, you sold for a loss until thirty days have passed. You can buy back similar stocks, or similar funds, but not the same ones during that thirty-day period.

The stock market has a great upward bias over the long term. Since World War II, the market has moved higher 80% of those calendar years. The DOW has returned more than 22,000%, annualized, over the past century, despite two world wars, regional conflicts throughout the world, terrorist attacks, depression, recession, the dot-com boom and bust between the mid 1990's and 2002, the American housing crisis of 2007-2009, bank bailouts, political mismanagement, and more.

Chapter 3

Technical Indicators and Reports

Successful investing involves the necessary merging of science, art, experience, and intuition. You can observe and interpret technical indicators, but they only reveal part of the story and must be confirmed by other observations and analyses.

Technical analysis, as it relates to the stock market, refers to methods of evaluating securities based on their market activity, and data generated by that activity. Details such as past prices, volume, and trends are logged and analyzed, with the goal of understanding future prices and directions. With the possible exception of candlestick analysis, to be explained later, indicators generally describe what the asset has been doing, not what it will be doing in the future.

Fundamental analysis attempts to determine the intrinsic value of a security. This might include financial statements, quarterly reports, and anything that affects the known value of a security. In essence, you are "looking under the hood" to see, and evaluate, important basics of a security. In the example of a stock, fundamental analysis seeks to determine if the stock's current price is appropriate, or does it undervalue or overvalue the stock.

There are literally hundreds of technical indicators available to investors. Which ones should you employ? Why? How many should you consider using? Answers to these types of questions depend on your goals, trading models, and methodologies.

I believe that "less is more." The more indicators you put on your charts, the more cluttered and unreadable they become. It is also not unusual to have contradictory indicators, especially when you evaluate trading in different time frames. And, since practically all indicators tell you what has happened in the past, don't you want to have a better idea of what might happen in the near future?

The other problem I have with indicators is philosophical and theoretical. The general question is, "Do indicators describe the stock market, or does the stock market describe the indicators?"

The market doesn't give a hoot what any of us think, and does whatever it wants. It is a vast collection of stocks that moves as these stocks move. These stocks move according to their earnings, future prospects, management decisions, dividends, and national and world events.

Indicators were developed in an attempt to explain what the market is doing. Investors needed a foundation, key, or code on which to base trading decisions. As people began to give these indicators credibility, traders began to trade with them. If you stand on the street in New York City, point and look up to the sky, notice the number of people who will stop and also look up to the sky. Using indicators has become a form of a collective self-fulfilling prophecy. That is, once traders began believing in these indicators, and what they think they represent, as a group they began trading off them in predictable patterns.

Listen to traders on Wall Street describe different indicators, percentages, averages, and prior price ranges in stocks and indexes. As traders believe in these statistical processes, and look to trade according to them, guess what: they appear to be effective (because many are doing the same thing). So, we have put indicators over stock charts, created meaning out of what we think we see, and now trade accordingly.

What I like to do is wait a short time to see if there are enough traders beginning to trade a predictable way, positive or negative, then get in front of them, and ride along. When the price gets to a point where I expect traders to become nervous, because of certain indicators, I try to take my profits ahead of them.

Later in this chapter, before I discuss three models to profitably trade stock index futures, I'll outline the political and economic issues that affect stock prices, and summarize the most important ones you should track. These issues affect present investor thinking and behavior. Current investor sentiment and activity are what count, and that is what we will use to make our trading decisions.

Measures of Central Tendency

The term "average" is perhaps the most-used basic technical term. Unfortunately, average has three traditional definitions, and is used in confusing and misleading ways when describing annual returns of securities, especially mutual funds.

The three main descriptions of average are mean, median, and mode. A mean average is used when we add the total of a group of numbers, then divide by the number in that group. For example, to determine what your average monthly investment production was for last year, you would list your monthly trading incomes, add them to get total income, and then divide by 12. That would be your average monthly trading income, based on using a mean score.

Median is more of a common average score. Again, you have a group of scores. You first rank-order them from highest to lowest. You then count to determine what the middle, or central score is. That is the median score.

Mode begins the same way. You rank-order a group of scores from highest to lowest, then find the score that appears most often. Among larger groups of scores, there will be duplicate scores, usually around the middle of the distribution. That score, which appears most often, is the mode. If you have two scores that appear the same number of times, the distribution is described as bi-modal.

You will see averages often described in terms of median scores. This is done to minimize the excessive influence extreme scores have on the mean. Here is an example. A homeless man is sitting on the sidewalk with a donation bowl in front of him. He is there for only part of a day, and gets the following donations: a nickel, a dime, a dime, a quarter, a quarter, and another quarter. Then a particularly generous woman stops by and puts a twenty-dollar bill in his bowl. That's it for the day. He counts out his fortunes, and concludes that he has received a total of twenty-one dollars through seven donations. His median average was about twenty-five cents (technically, since there were three quarters you should statistically adjust this, but close enough), his mode average was twenty-five cents, but his mean average was three dollars. Clearly, the median and mode are better descriptors of his average donation for the day.

How does the financial system, particularly the mutual fund industry, regularly mislead us? When a company describes its average five- or ten-year return, say ten percent, there should be an asterisk. Follow it down; it should say "annualized." If you are not familiar with the term, it means you would get this return *only* if you bought on the first day, and held for the full period. Annualized includes the magic of compounding.

There is a simple formula for figuring this out yourself; it's called the "rule of 72." If you know the rate of return you can expect, you divide 72 by that rate to determine the length of time needed for this security to double in value. For example, if you earn a return of six percent per year, your asset will double in twelve years. If you earn ten percent, it will double in 7.2 years.

Let's return to a ten-year annualized return of ten percent per year. At ten percent per year, the company is indicating that this asset doubled in ten years. *But*, it earned an average of 7.2% every year, *not* ten percent every year. And, the longer the annualized period, the greater is the magnification of actual annual returns.

Look for the term "average annual return." This means they added the returns from each of the past years (ex: ten), and divided by that ten years to get a mean average return. If this asset doubled in ten years, they should describe its return as "an average annual return of 7.2%."

Moving Averages

There are two basic types of averages: simple and exponential. Their numbers represent periods of time. A simple moving average (SMA) is a mean average of closing prices over the numbered time period specified. A twenty-period SMA could be twenty weeks, twenty days, twenty four-hour periods, twenty one-hour periods, twenty fifteen-minute periods, or other time frames.

The exponential moving average (EMA) adds incremental amounts to the scores as the average approaches the end of its duration. This provides increasing emphasis to scores as you get closer to the current score, reflecting more weight to the latest scores. It represents different numbered periods the same as the SMA.

Traders more commonly use the 200-day SMA, the 50-day SMA, and the 20-day SMA. Days obviously reflect trading days, so a 20-day SMA would cover most of the last calendar month. These three averages provide a longer-term, middle-term, and shorter-term view of market prices and activity.

A popular term using averages is the "death cross." This means in an advancing market, where you have long positions, planning on increasing prices, the 20-day line crosses under the 50-day line. (Traders use any of the common averages in pairs to evaluate the market.) The obvious concern is that the shorter-term price average is moving lower than the longer-term average, suggesting a downward turn in the market. If this is the case, you may want to close your long positions. You can also experiment with shorter periods, such as comparing five-day and ten-day simple moving averages.

The other side of this situation is the "Golden Cross." This is when the short-term average, such as a 20-day SMA moves above the longer-term average, usually a 50-day SMA. If you are trading for the market to rise, this is positive, as it shows the shorter-term trend moving above the longer-term trend.

MACD

The moving average convergence divergence (MACD) is a trend-following momentum indicator. It is designed to show the relationship of prices between two moving averages. To calculate, the twenty-six-day exponential moving average (EMA) is subtracted from the 12-day EMA. A signal line is then calculated to function as a trigger for buy and sell signals. This is a 9-day EMA of the MACD, which is plotted on top of the MACD.

If the MACD falls below the signal line, that is a bearish signal, and you need to monitor your position to see if it may soon be time to sell, or possibly go short. If the MACD rises above the signal line, that is a bullish signal, and suggests that the market might continue higher.

If the MACD rises dramatically, where the shorter-term moving average moves away from the longer-term average, that suggests that the equity you are monitoring may be overbought, and will move back toward more normal price levels. If the price of the equity you are trading moves in a direction opposite the MACD, the current trend may be coming to an end.

Traders watch the position of the MACD relative to the zero line. If the MACD moves above zero, the short-term average is above the long-term average, suggesting upward momentum. If the MACD moves below zero, the price is probably moving lower. The zero line is often viewed as an indicator of support and resistance for the equity's price. The MACD is most useful as a confirmation indicator of a trading decision made on the basis of other factors.

RSI

The Relative Strength Index (RSI) is another technical momentum indicator. It is calculated by the following formula: RSI = 100 - 100/(1 + RS). This attempts to compare recent price gains to recent price losses, to determine overbought to oversold conditions. To do this, RSI is defined as the average of "x" days of up closes/the average of "x" days of down closes. You don't need to know the complexities of this formula.

The range of the RSI is zero to one hundred. If the RSI rises to seventy or above, it may be getting ready to pull back. If it falls near thirty or below, the equity may be oversold, and ready to move higher. The indicator has horizontal lines at thirty and seventy, making it easier to read and monitor. This is another indicator that is best used in an effort to find confirmation of a trading decision.

The number of days used in this formula can be plugged in at the trader's discretion. It can vary depending on changing conditions and volatility. Ten to fifteen days (two to three weeks) might be a reasonable starting point.

It is important to remember that markets can stay overvalued, or undervalued, for weeks or months. That is why momentum indicators should only be used to seek confirmation based on other factors and information.

Stochastic Oscillator

This is a difficult indicator to explain, let alone understand. The stochastic oscillator is benchmarked to one hundred, as a way to normalize the data. When you do that, it is described as an oscillator. This means that the indicator values are limited to a particular range relative to the starting point. This is usually the difference, or the ratio, between today's price and the price x number of days ago. Sensitivity of the oscillator to market movements can be reduced by adjusting the time period, or taking a simple moving average (SMA) of the result.

The theory of this indicator is that prices tend to close near their high, on a daily basis, in an up-trending market, and close near their daily low in a down-trending market. When %K crosses through %D, a transaction signal is given. Trading platforms give you options for entering numbers in the formula; many traders prefer to use 12,3,3.

The formula is: %K = 100 {(C - L14)/(H14 - L14)}

C = the most recent closing price

L14 = the low of the prior 14 trading sessions

H14 = the highest trading price of the same prior 14 trading sessions

%D = 3-period moving average of %K

This momentum indicator is the least lagging, because it focuses on speed of change, not simply the trend. This is the one I favor to use with other indicators, especially candlesticks. You don't need to know these calculations; stochastics move as a line in a chart, with eighty suggesting overbought, and twenty suggesting oversold. You will see more information about how this is expressed in later chapters.

Candlesticks

This is the core of how we will trade. Candlesticks are the best indicators for describing *current* investor sentiment and behavior, and are the most revealing and helpful to trading e-mini stock index futures. Candlesticks also work on any time frame, so you can break down a daily chart into any smaller time frame and the signals work just as well.

Around four hundred years ago, Japanese rice traders developed this system to help them understand trader behavior and pricing, in buying and selling rice. Those who used and fine-tuned this system became extraordinarily wealthy. This approach was not translated and "Westernized" until the 1990's when Steve Nison began to use and write about this in the United States.

Others, including Stephen Bigelow, also wrote books and adapted candlesticks for trading stocks and other products.

Candlesticks have been slow to catch on. Some have viewed them as too difficult to understand and use, too technical, too many patterns that become confusing, etc. That is not the case. You will be introduced to them here, then a select group will be explained in later chapters, as will their applications to simplify and amplify your trading. I have been trading e-mini futures with candlesticks part-time for several years, with a very high trade success rate, and consistent profits of several thousand dollars a month. You can also do this.

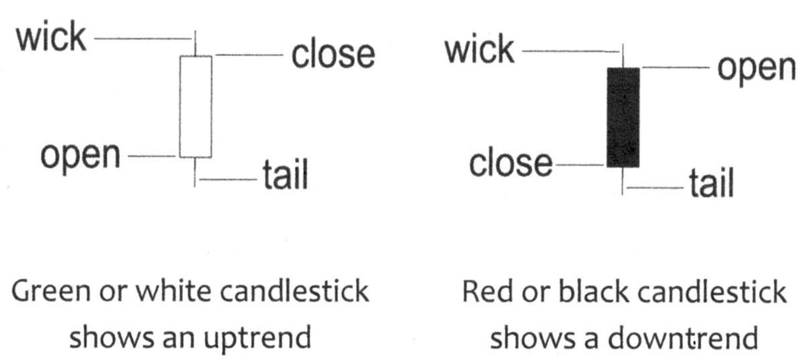

Green or white candlestick shows an uptrend

Red or black candlestick shows a downtrend

A green or white candlestick shows that the price of the entity you are trading has finished higher for the time period the candlestick represents. This could be any period from one minute to one month. We'll use one day as the time, and one of the e-mini stock index futures as the entity. The bottom of the positive candle is the price where the index opened that day, and the top closed end shows the price where the index closed at the end of that day.

A red or black candlestick is the opposite. The top closed end of the candle is the price where the index opened, and the bottom closed end is where it closed at the end of the day. Candlestick charts are color-paired as green-red (up and down), or white-black (up and down).

The "wick" at the top of any candle represents how far the index moved up that day, whether an up or down candle. The "tail" at the bottom of either candle shows how low the price moved that day. Obviously, the longer the candle, and/or the longer the wick and tail, the greater is the price range for that day. A longer candle, therefore, shows greater price volatility.

The use of candlesticks will improve your trading outcomes. Upcoming chapters describe candlestick patterns in ways that will enable you to become a better trader, especially when the market appears ready to change direction. Through different time frames, you will be able to see what other traders are doing, and have a better sense of what they are thinking and feeling. Seeing and knowing how other traders are reacting to price movements gives you a distinct and powerful advantage.

Government-related Reports

Keeping apprised of economic and governmental reports around the world is important, as the U.S. stock markets move on international news. And, since news is essentially instantaneous, it can have an immediate effect on stock and futures prices. One excellent, and free, resource is: http://www.investing.com/economic-calendar/. This source includes international releases, as well as such events as speeches by members of the FOMC (Federal Open Market Committee, aka "the Fed"). It lists the name of the report, actual numbers from the most recent report, the expected numbers for the current report, and, after release, the actual numbers. Significance for possible market influence and volatility is expressed through what looks like a gray face of a bull. Volatility is expressed by showing one, two, or three bullish icons. These icons represent only the level of market influence, not expected direction. There are other sites available for free, or for a monthly fee.

The following is an alphabetical list of reports, indicators, and events that have varying influences on all U.S. markets. Reference for these is investopedia.com. The most important ones will be listed first, then a summary mention of some of the less-influential reports. Dozens of economic indicators and surveys are released every week; these lists are not inclusive.

"Beige Book" -- This is released two Wednesdays before every FOMC meeting, eight times each year. It contains summaries and anecdotal information regarding all regional activity. Since this doesn't contain new data, it has limited current affect on markets. But, it does include language that may hint of the FOMC's attitudes and possible future decisions.

Consumer Confidence Index (CCI) -- This is released the last Tuesday of each month. It is formed from surveying some 5,000 households, and is designed to gauge consumer financial health, spending power, and confidence.

Consumer Price Index (CPI) -- The CPI is released around the middle of each month, and reports prices of many common products. It is used to determine the health of the economy and inflation trends.

Crude Oil Inventories -- This is released every Wednesday (sometimes on Thursday because of holidays or other scheduling issues). It describes inventories of all distillate products. If inventories surprise to the downside, crude oil prices may rise, good news for oil-related stocks, but bad news for some consumer stocks. Oil is priced in dollars, and there is a complex relationship between crude oil and U.S. and international markets.

Durable Goods Report -- This is released on or around the 20th of each month. A volatile number, this describes data on new items with a useful life of three years or more. It is a broad assessment of consumer behavior and the economy, and tends to move with new housing numbers, and business upgrades and expansion.

Employment Report -- This is a major survey report of households and employers, and is closely followed by market watchers. It is released at 8:30 a.m. eastern time, on the first Friday of each month. The number of jobs created can indicate whether the economy is strengthening or weakening. This report is heavily revised after release, so it tends to show current economic conditions rather than predicting future conditions. If the report is considerably different than predicted, especially if significantly fewer jobs were created, that can send the market lower. The FOMC looks closely at this report for both indicators of the economy, and suggestions of inflation if the numbers are quite high. Markets usually move sharply, often in both directions, when this report is released.

Existing Home Sales -- This report is released by the National Association of Realtors during the last week of each month. It describes the number of existing home sales closed during the survey month, by geographic regions of the country, and the average sale price. It describes consumer behavior, and is a leading indicator in areas related to home improvements and furnishings.

FOMC Speeches -- If the Federal Reserve (FOMC) is open to raising or lowering interest rates, that type of activity usually moves the market. Observers also look for clues of future fed policy by dissecting speeches given by FOMC members. Be aware of these speeches, as there are sometimes sharp moves in market prices.

Gross Domestic Product (GDP) -- This describes the market value of all goods and services produced by the economy during the period measured. It is sometimes referred to as the “godfather” of the indicator world. The advance release is made four weeks after each quarter ends; the final release is made three months after a quarter ends. The GDP is very detailed and comprehensive, and incorporates data from other reports. This report says the most about the health of the U.S. economy, and its release will usually move markets.

New Housing Starts -- This is released on, or around, the 17th of each month, and its data describes building permits, new housing starts, and new housing completions throughout the U.S. These numbers are seldom surprising in a meaningful way, but do suggest how related and supportive industry stocks will fare in the near future.

Jobless Claims Report -- Released every Thursday before the market opens, this shows the number of first-time filings for state jobless claims throughout the country. Weekly results can be quite volatile, so results are often reported as four-week averages. The stock market often reacts to reports that are not within the expected range, as jobs reflect economic activity which influences stock valuations.

Job Openings and Labor Turnover Survey (JOLTS) -- This report collects monthly data from a wide variety of employers, and is summarized by region and industry. This data aids in the analysis of business cycles, industry retention rates, and economic research by industry.

Producer Price Index (PPI) -- This report is released at 8:30 a.m. Eastern Time during the second or third week of each month. It is produced by the Bureau of Labor Statistics (BLS), and shows trends within the wholesale and commodities markets and manufacturing industries. It includes all physical goods-producing industries in the U.S. economy, so is a good descriptor of the U.S.

economy and is a meaningful predictor of the Consumer Price Index (CPI).

Purchasing Managers Index (PMI) -- The PMI is compiled through surveys to members of a non-profit group of those engaged in purchasing and supply management professions. Their members total some 400 throughout the country, chosen to represent geographic and industry diversification. The PMI is released on the first work day of the month, and reports on the prior month's activity, so is very timely. A reading of fifty or higher reflects positively on manufacturing and the economy as a whole.

Retail Sales Report -- This report tracks the value of merchandise sold to consumers, and is closely watched by investors and economists. It is released at 8:30 a.m., Eastern Time, on or around the 13th of each month, and covers data from the prior month. This report is influential and closely followed, as it can shed much light on the U.S. economy. It can also be suggestive of inflationary pressures, and might influence the Federal Reserve's interest rate policy.

Some of the other reports that might influence the market include the Business Outlook Survey, Consumer Credit Report, Employee Cost Index, Factory Orders, Industrial Production, Money Supply, Mutual Fund Flows, Personal Income, and the U.S. Trade Balance.

About two dozen reports have been summarized; there is obviously a plethora of information available. And these are only those in the U.S. China, Japan, and Europe, among others can also move the markets, though many of these events, and initial market reactions, occur when most of us are sleeping.

If you trade in the morning, you should always look at the business headlines, and review the economic calendar to get the day's schedule before you begin trading. Mornings work very well for collecting smaller profits with the short-term trading model described in Chapter 8.

Chapter 4

Psychological and Practical Issues in Trading

It's not what happens to you, but how you react to it that matters. - - Epictetus

Since trading and investing involve both cognitive and emotional thinking, it is important to understand how the brain functions.

There are two distinct aspects of the human brain: cognitive and emotional. In the cognitive area, the cerebral cortex is a thin layer of gray matter that covers the surface of both cerebral hemispheres. The neocortex is a part of the mammalian brain. In the human brain, it is the largest part of the cerebral cortex. The cerebral cortex is responsible for all processes of sensual perception, spatial reasoning, thought, sleep, memory, and learning. It is the foundation for social abilities, language, problem solving, and all advanced motor functions, including generation of motor commands.

The emotional aspect is based in the limbic system. This system is a complex set of brain structures located on both sides of the thalamus, right under the cerebrum, near the center of the human brain. It is not a separate system, but a collection of structures including the olfactory bulbs, hippocampus, amygdala, fornix, mammillary body, limbic cortex, limbic midbrain areas, and others.

The limbic system supports a variety of functions including epinephrine flow, emotion, behavior, motivation, long-term memory, and olfaction. Emotional life is largely housed in the limbic system, and it plays a major role in the original formation of memories. It influences the endocrine system and the autonomic nervous system, and is highly interconnected with the brain's pleasure center. Those who lose cognitive control, and act impulsively and emotionally, are sometimes described as using their "lizard brain" (an emotional primal response), particularly if their behavior is linked to criminal or drug-related activity.

If you are invested in the market, and it is rising, your potential profits (on paper) also rise. This will stimulate your brain's pleasure center (limbic system). Therefore, that part of your brain can override the cognitive, disciplined part. This explains why, ultimately, people often end up losing the profits they thought they were going to get; they held on rather than sell and take profits.

In our daily lives, we know that emotions can alter our perceptions and decision-making, especially if we experience certain anxieties. Many of you may be familiar with some of the more-common defense mechanisms that may come into play. Let's review a few.

"Denial" is the most basic defense mechanism. We simply tell ourselves that what we see, think, or feel is not true; not real. When confronted with opinions or facts we don't want to acknowledge, we simply ignore them as untrue or insignificant. The successful trader must be accurately insightful, confident enough to accept unpleasant facts, and mature enough to be objective about himself or herself.

"Rationalization" is something we are all familiar with. We might agree with the facts about ourselves, or a situation we have created, but we "blow it off" with comments that explain it away. That way, we deny responsibility, and don't have to engage in any corrective behaviors.

"Projection" is the misattribution of a person's thoughts, feelings or behaviors onto another person who doesn't have them. We blame others for these when, in fact, we are the one who has them. Projection usually exists in people who lack insight and the ability to acknowledge these features in themselves.

"Repression" is the unconscious blocking of unacceptable feelings, thoughts and impulses. Since you are not consciously aware, you often have little control over these. These usually come from earlier experiences we do not want to bring into awareness because they are unpleasant.

"Displacement" is the redirecting of unpleasant thoughts, feelings, or behaviors from one person or object onto another. This usually results when one cannot respond to the irritating source, so the person takes it out on another. An example is an employee who is angry at his or her boss, but cannot say anything for fear of being fired. So, when that person gets home, he/she yells at the spouse or kicks the family dog. That way, release is found from the internal pressure. Of course, this only exacerbates the problem.

Those of you who are, or aspire to be, successful traders need to be open, self-aware, accept responsibility for your decisions and behaviors, and be willing and able to accept facts, and profit from your experiences.

For traders, the feelings of "fear" and "greed" can taint your perceptions and judgment. Equity and bond markets move on these emotions. The famous investor, Warren Buffet, is known for saying, "Buy when others are fearful, and sell when others are greedy." This reflects the sound trading philosophy of "buy low, sell high."

For the individual trader, anxiety can be paralyzing, especially if you have experienced negative trades. In this situation, it is easy to get into what Albert Ellis, the famous behavioral psychologist, called "stinkin' thinkin'." When we engage in a decision and behavior that has a negative outcome, whether our fault or not, we tend to internalize this outcome as not only our fault, but, because of this, we generalize our assessment into a belief that we are a failure as a person. Remember to objectively evaluate your decisions and behaviors, and seek to improve your approach. Do not generalize into believing or feeling that there is something personally wrong with you.

Feelings related to greed can also be problematic. Humans tend to overvalue their good fortune as a tribute to their brilliance, while explaining away their losses as bad luck. No one wants to think they are stupid. We feel worse about losing $300 than we feel good about winning $300. Trading involves making intelligent decisions that have the highest probability of success.

Trading is NOT gambling. Ultimately, when gambling, the house always wins. Why? Gamblers cannot stand to win. Their thrill is the comeback, trying to dig themselves out of the financial hole they have created. People can win; the problem is most cannot take their winnings home. They continue on, losing what they brought with them, plus what they won, and often too much more than that. As a trader, keep your wits about you, and disavow any interest in such self-destructive behavior as doubling down if you have a losing trade.

The models in this book are specific with a high probability of success, and limited in risk. If you follow the guidelines in the coming chapters, stay objective and under control, you will be very satisfied with the outcome. You will be making profits, *but* do not get greedy and put too much capital at risk. Stay steady and consistent.

Gambling - - the sure way of getting nothing for something. - - Wilson Mizner

Present vs. the Future

I spent most of my adult life focused on assessing, evaluating, and treating human behavior, and teaching these principles to undergraduate and graduate university students. Students would learn the history, theory, and philosophies of these areas, but my focus was on them. Each of these students was the instrument of application, because information and principles taught to them were naturally filtered through their individual personalities.

We are shaped by our experiences, and we interpret and filter new information through our belief systems, self-concepts, biases, prejudices, and all other personal and human factors that make each of us distinct. My goal was to teach self-awareness, so each student would understand how they were interpreting and filtering the information offered, how that would affect them individually, and how they would behave and apply this information as a unique person.

When I conducted offender evaluations, the purpose was to describe the offender's current mental status and behavior, and whether or not there appeared to be specific current problems or issues. But, the real goal was to use this current information as a basis to make predictions about future behavior, such as how he would function in a parole situation. In most areas of life, where assessments and evaluations are conducted, we are asked to analyze and interpret what we see in the present, but use current information to predict the future. Therein lies the rub.

Whether human assessment, or economic and stock market assessment, the first problem is differences of opinion as to what we see in the present. Turn on a business news television station and listen to the "talking heads." There will often be two experts providing their analysis of current economic and market conditions, and their opinions as to what will happen in the future. Almost always, they have opposing points of view. That is why it is usually a good idea to avoid witnessing that activity; you only get confused.

The best anyone can do is analyze and provide forms of "if, then" observations. For offenders, I would provide a clinical assessment of his or her current status and functioning, then propose some "if, then" scenarios. Since no one can predict the future for themselves, or any other person, it is important to emphasize the environment. If an offender leaves prison, and encounters situational cluster of factors "A," he will likely react one way. If, however, he leaves prison and encounters situational cluster of factors "B," he will behave a different way. The key is what he encounters in his environment, and the personal choices he makes to adapt or cope.

For traders, the principles are the same. You are the "instrument of trading application," so you must thoroughly, and honestly, know yourself. You evaluate current economic and political conditions, but you don't know what will happen in the future, or how the markets will behave. So, as you set yourself up to trade, and develop some optional approaches to trading, you formulate your own set of "if, then" principles to prepare yourself for all that the market might throw at you. The three models in this book provide very workable situations where probabilities of success are high, and risk is limited.

The lack of money is the root of all evil. - - Mark Twain

Risk Tolerance, Age, and Experience

Part of knowing yourself, and preparing to be a trader, is your age, purpose for trading, risk tolerance, and prior investing experience. There are tools available for such self-assessment.

One example is an investor questionnaire from Vanguard (Vanguard.com). There are 11 questions; I'll just list each question with a summary of what it is, without the foils (answer options). You can respond to this questionnaire on their web site, and get a general response profile. This will help you understand your own risk tolerance and aptitude for trading.

1. I plan to begin taking money from my investments in ...(number of years)

2. As I withdraw money from these investments, I plan to spend it over a period of...(number of years)
3. When making a long-term investment, I plan to keep the money invested for...(number of years)
4. From September, 2008 through November, 2008, stocks lost over 31%. If I owned a stock investment that lost about 31% in three months, I would... (how much would you sell, or buy?)
5. Generally, I prefer investments with little or no fluctuation in value, and I'm willing to accept the lower return associated with these investments... (level of agreement with this statement)
6. During market declines, I tend to sell portions of my riskier assets and invest the money in safer assets...(level of agreement)
7. I would invest in a mutual fund based solely on a brief conversation with a friend, co-worker or relative...(level of agreement)
8. From September, 2008, through October, 2008, bonds lost nearly 4%. If I owned a bond investment that lost almost 4% in two months, I would...(how much would you hold or sell?)
9. The chart below shows the greatest one-year loss, and highest one-year gain on three different hypothetical investments of $10,000. Given the potential gain or loss in any one year, I would invest my money in...(addresses level of volatility you are comfortable with)

10. My current and future income sources (for example salary, Social Security, pensions) are... (level of stability)
11. When it comes to investing in stock or bond mutual funds (or individual stocks and bonds), I would describe myself as...(level of experience)

Attitude is a little thing that makes a big difference. - - Winston Churchill

Why do You Want to be a Trader?

Now that you've read this far, have you more clarity as to why you want to be a trader in the first place? Are you bored? Looking for new challenges? Like to gamble? (Not good.) Need the money? Looking to leave a family legacy?

At the beginning of the book, I wrote about how I wanted to leave assets and a model for making money as a personal legacy to my family. That is only part of the story. There is also a need to be creative and challenged.

Erik Erikson developed a theory of psychosocial development that has eight stages. Stage 7 is generativity vs. stagnation. The basic virtue is Care. Age is adulthood, 40 - 65. Stage 8 is ego integrity vs. despair. Basic virtue is Wisdom. Age is 66+.

Before beginning this book, I reflected on my life. I was fortunate to have a very productive and successful career, but also continued to need intellectual challenges and activities when I retired. Age is not a number; it is an attitude, a capacity to produce value based on years of learning and experience. Many of you may have years of productivity and seasoning, but want to continue to learn and engage in challenging activities. Certainly, the virtues of care and wisdom apply to mature adults, as does the need for generativity and ego integrity.

I have greatly enjoyed the challenges and success associated with the development of these three models. I hope you will share the same purpose and enthusiasm as you read through this book.

Chapter 5

Trading E-mini Stock Index Futures

In trading and investing, it's not just how good your decisions are, it's how bad they aren't. - - Dennis B. Anderson

Before you begin trading, you need to review your asset allocation. Do you have a good balance between stocks and stock funds; bonds and bond funds; possibly real estate, commodities, international equities; and enough cash for emergencies? The other balance is how we allocate consumable income. We should always save for the future and retirement, and have assets available for unpredictable expenses such as a medical emergency, a new car, a new furnace, a special vacation, or perhaps to help adult children who experience a personal financial tragedy. And we should responsibly accumulate assets to enjoy ourselves on a regular basis.

So then the question becomes, "Where are you going to get the money to set up your trading account?" You will need at least $10,000 - $15,000 to establish a margin account with enough flexibility and resources to trade e-mini stock index futures. This is a high-risk, high-reward activity that requires adequate capital, and you should use only money you can afford to lose. It requires attention, discipline, patience, and a belief in what you are doing.

You need to begin by selecting a broker, or firm, and a trading platform that effectively allows you to trade e-mini stock index futures. The platform allows you to make all your trades, monitor your status on all positions, and track your capital expenditures and accumulations. The broker, or firm, manages your account, answers questions, prepares tax statements, and provides indicators and resources to support your trading activities.

There are many certified firms that provide these services. You have no doubt seen some of their advertisements on television. They can be identified and reviewed through an internet search engine, and you can analyze their information and make direct contact with them as you determine your choice. It is easier to use only one broker, so be sure the one you select provides all the trading options and services you need, especially if you wish to trade a broader variety of equities or bonds.

I use Ameritrade and their Think or Swim platform. Their staff are excellent; you can call or email them to get the information or services you need. They have an extensive amount of trading tool options and resources, and flexibility to research or organize yourself as you see fit. And, of course, you can arrange or colorize your trading platform in many configurations.

Platforms vary by provider because they have different philosophies and programmers. Generally, here are a few details to help you get started. After making your decision, you go to your provider's web site and download their trading platform. After you are settled with that, you might want to explore their "help" sections to minimize trial and error.

You have to set up your grid and determine how many e-mini stock indexes you want on your screen at the same time. I like to have two at a time, because I often trade different indexes at the same time on my larger accounts. At the beginning, however, I suggest you have only one e-mini index on your screen to minimize confusion. There will also be space, perhaps on the left side, for prices and other means of monitoring the market. The other side might show trading activity in the index(s) you have on your screen. Account information and trading screen options are usually at the top of the screen.

Your default settings may be close to what you need. If not, set your background (I use black, but there are numerous options), choose candlesticks as your standard indicator (I suggest red and green), and locate where you select the index you wish to follow/trade. There will also be a place where you can select the time frame; that could be one minute to one week. There are about eight time choices you can use to monitor market activity.

The real adventure is finding, and placing on your charts, the indicators you wish to use. You may see a tab for "add study," or something similar. That will likely give you a main menu listing. Let's say you want to add an exponential moving average. There should be a "moving average" option. Click on that and look for "exponential moving average." Click that, and put it on your chart. It will default to some number, often something like 9-period. You will need to get into the details of that, select the period length you want, then select the color you want for this moving average line. You will want different colors for different indicator lines, and pick ones that will be distinct from each other. Be sure to be consistent in your choices, so all charts will look the same. There are many colors and shades to choose from.

When you are selecting an e-mini stock index future to trade, the menu will give you options you may not notice. For example, /ES is the symbol for the S & P 500 e-mini futures index. It may show as nothing but /ES, or it may have one or two additional codes after it. These represent different quarterly futures contracts, and are linked to different quarters. Be sure to select the correct one (the current futures that will expire at the end of the current quarter), or you could have an open position in another category of futures contract you may lose track of.

Scaling

When setting up your platform, explore all it can do, and take nothing for granted. Chart scaling is important to notice. On the side of the chart will be numbers that represent the range of value of the index you have on your screen, as it is reflected in the time period you have chosen. These value ranges change as your time frame is changed, so the size of the candlesticks in each time frame will also change. This can be confusing if you forget about differences in scaling.

Linear, or interval, scaling is a scale where differences between numerical numbers and time are always equal. So, the difference between four and five is the same as the difference between 536 and 537. Trading platforms are normally set to linear scaling.

You may have seen a chart that uses logarithmic scaling. In this form, calculations are indicated as percentage of change between numbers, so the higher you go up the scale the more compressed the numbers are. Scales and meaning are changed considerably when you compare the two over time. If you are looking at comparative scaling, be sure they are both linear scaling, or both logarithmic scaling.

Before you use real money, you will need to practice trading. Your trading platform provider should have a "paper or practice account" option available, and will deposit a sufficient amount of "paper money" for you to trade. That type of account uses artificial dollars for simulating the same trades and amounts as you will use when you put actual money at risk. It is very different when you use real money, as opposed to paper money, and you must practice as if the money you are trading is actually your savings. This practice trading will also help you become familiar with the trading platform, reducing anxiety. Study the three models in later chapters, and practice trading for several months before risking your money.

The CME Group (Chicago Mercantile Exchange), and the Chicago Board of Trade, are the most diverse derivatives marketplace offering the widest range of futures and options products for risk management. The CME also has offices in New York City and London, and its influence is felt in markets throughout the world.

Individual trading platforms are linked to the CME, which transacts and processes your trading requests. You can get on the CME email list, and receive notices and updates, although these seldom affect your trading of e-mini stock index futures.

Futures expire after the third Friday of each quarter. The next quarter's futures become listed around Monday of the expiration week so, if you have open (active) positions you will need to close them that week. If you wish, you can buy the next quarter's futures at that time. Futures prices begin each quarterly period lower than they are close to expiration. This makes sense, as there is more risk concerning the value of a futures contract that expires three months from now, as opposed to one that expires a week from now. For example the /ES, e-mini futures for the S & P 500, may be three or more points lower at the beginning of a quarterly contract than at the end. So, if you replace an expiring contract with a new one, compare prices at the time you sell and buy, and you will be close to the same situation. Be careful not to mix quarterly time periods.

Margin

Buying and selling e-mini stock index futures is carried out by the use of margins, essentially using borrowed money. This is much like buying a thirty-thousand-dollar car with three thousand down. You drive away in a nice new vehicle, but could only afford to spend three thousand dollars. The loan agency is holding the title, and obviously expects you to make good on your debt should something happen. With margin, you can make much greater profits through each trading transaction, but it also means you have a risk of equal losses if the trade moves against you.

Buying and selling a stock is different. It is a straightforward transaction. To buy one hundred shares of a ten-dollar stock, I give the broker one thousand dollars, plus a trading fee, and I now own those one hundred shares. If they increase ten percent in value and I sell, I receive eleven hundred back, a ten percent profit. But, if the stock drops ten percent to nine dollars, I receive nine hundred dollars for my shares, a ten percent loss. Trading on margin is much different.

You first have to establish a cash account at your brokerage. The minimum amount (at least two thousand dollars) may vary, depending on what you are planning to trade.

The maintenance margin will be higher, usually between twenty-five percent and forty percent of the total market value of the securities in the margin account. If you buy too many securities for the amount in your margin account, and/or the value of your securities has dropped below an acceptable maintenance margin level, you may get a margin call to deposit additional funds. If you do not act in time, usually a day or two, the brokerage will sell enough of your existing assets, at whatever is current market value, to bring your left-over assets in acceptable alignment with margin requirements. There will be no selective selling; they will close whatever positions they want (remember, this is considered their money), and you will not have any input. If you are trading e-mini futures worth one hundred dollars a point, your account balance can change rapidly.

Obviously, to protect yourself from such a position, you need to have sufficient capital in your account, trade carefully, use stop losses in the beginning, and don't buy more positions than what your account can cover, should they decline in value before you can respond. Don't be too concerned by all this; the upcoming trading models take these issues into consideration and, with proper discipline, you will be just fine, enjoying your profits.

The first rule of holes: When you're in one, stop digging. - - Molly Ivins

Trading Five E-mini Stock Index Futures

Trading normal-sized futures contracts requires a great deal of capital, and is best left for institutional and hedge fund managers. The e-mini stock index futures contract allows us to trade the same index, with about one-fifth the capital. Margin requirements are different for each of the five indexes, and will vary according to the overall market situation and the volatility of each index.

As mentioned in the Introduction, these are the five e-mini index futures you will be trading. The ES (trade symbol /ES) has the same composition as the S & P 500 Index, representing 500 of the largest corporations in the U.S. The NQ (trade symbol /NQ), represents the NASDAQ 100 Index. The YM (trade symbol /YM) represents the DOW 30 Stock Index. The EMD (trade symbol /EMD) represents the S & P Midcap 400 Stock Index. And the TF (trade symbol /TF) represents the Russell 2000 Small Cap Index.

The /TF was priced at $100 a point until December 5, 2016, when it was reduced by half to $50 a point. This reduced trading fees by about sixty cents per trade. All discussion about trading during the writing of this book includes the /TF priced at $100 a point. The following information, including future tables reflects the reduced price of the /TF futures. As you plan your trades, remember to price the /TF at $50 a point.

A "tick" size is the smallest part of an e-mini index that can be traded. For the /ES, a tick is .25 of a point. This tick has a value of $12.50. So, each one-point move in the /ES is worth $50. Margin requirements are about $5000 to trade one /ES contract.

One tick for the /NQ is .25 of a point. This tick has a value of $5. So, each one-point move in the /NQ has a value of $20. Margin requirements are about $4800 to trade one /NQ contract.

One tick for the /YM is one point. This tick has a value of $5. So, each one-point move in the /YM has a value of $5. Margin requirements are about $4100 to trade one / YM contract.

One tick for the /EMD is .1 of a point. This tick has a value of $10. So, each one-point move in the /EMD has a value of $100. Margin requirements are about $7400 to trade one /EMD contract.

One tick for the /TF is .1 of a point. This tick has a value of $5. So, each one-point move in the /TF has a value of $50. Margin requirements are about $5100 to trade one /TF contract.

Types of Trading Orders

When we think of trading, we naturally think of profits. That is usually first defined as buy low, sell higher. That is referred to as going long the market. There are several ways you can buy, or go long, the market. The basic order is simply a market order. Once you click buy, your order is immediately filled at whatever current market price the system can find. Remember, index markets are a zero-sum game; you can't buy unless someone on the other side wants to sell at whatever price you are willing to pay. If you enter a market order when the index is very volatile, you may pay a price much lower, or higher than you anticipated. That is referred to as a form of slippage, something you want to avoid. Of course, you have the same problem if you simply enter a market sell order. You might get considerably less for your position than you had planned.

You can be more specific about a price you are willing to pay by entering a limit buy order. Let's say you have been monitoring the trading range, and maybe the market has dipped lower a bit. If you place a limit buy order a few points lower than the current price, you will get your lower buy price if a seller is offering his/her contract for sale at that price. Putting in a limit sell order works the same way. You specify the price you are willing to accept as a sale, and you wait for a willing buyer.

Long trades have been summarized above. You can also use short trades. If you think prices are too high, or that economic conditions are such that a drop in the market seems fairly certain, you can go short. Using a margin account, you enter a limit short position by borrowing an index futures contract from your broker (this happens automatically), then selling it. When the price (hopefully) drops to your target level, you buy back the contract with a limit buy, or buy to cover your short, to replace the contract you earlier borrowed from your broker, and enjoy your profit.

Sometimes price moves against you, and you have to buy back the contract you borrowed at a higher price than you paid, thus absorbing a loss. When you go long, your losses can be great if the market drops significantly. And when you go short and the market turns against you and goes up, your losses are unlimited. Neither is a good place to be.

Whether long or short, when you have an active (open) position, you can enter a protective stop loss order. More detail on this will appear later, but as a simple explanation, if you go long, you put a limit sell order a few points below your buy price, so your losses are limited if the contract price moves lower than where you bought. When you short, you put a limit buy order a few points above your short sell price, so if the market turns higher, above your buy point, you are stopped out, and your losses are limited. In extreme and sudden market moves, traders sometimes do not get execution at the price they wanted, but a few points beyond their limit point. Generally though, with e-minis, you will get the price you wanted.

A trailing stop is an order to close a long or short position a certain number of ticks, or points, below an advancing position, or above a dropping short position, thereby locking in some profit. Let's say you are long the /ES, and you bought at the price of 2100. The price moves up to 2110. You would like to assure five points of profit from this trade, so you enter a sell order at 2105. If the price moves back down to 2105, you would be stopped out, but would have a profit of five points, in this case $250. But, if the price continues higher, maybe to 2120, you could move your stop to 2115, locking in fifteen points of profit.

Trading platforms have trailing stops that adjust automatically, if you prefer that method. If your index is steadily rising above your buy price, you enter a trailing stop of a certain number of points. If the price advances a few points, the trailing stop will rise the same number of points. If the price retreats, the trailing price will stay at its last position; it will not retreat with the price. So, if the price moves low enough, you will automatically be stopped out, but locking in whatever profit you managed to accrue.

Order Duration

Duration refers to the length of time you want to keep your order active for execution. If you enter an order and walk away, and it is not executed that day, it will automatically be withdrawn at the end of the day (daily expiration), and will never be executed. If you have an active, or open, position, and enter a limit order at a specific price, but it is not filled that day, it too will vanish at the end of the day, because a longer duration was not specified.

There are as many as seven types of orders that specify time periods before expiration and withdrawal. For e-mini futures, there are basically two types: the automatic daily expiration mentioned above, or GTC, meaning good till cancelled. With GTC, your order and price stay in place until filled, or you personally cancel or amend the order. You may decide to reenter the order at a different price.

Markets and Times of Activity

The name Bourse originally referred to the French stock market, but today some refer to all foreign stock markets, or exchanges as Bourses. The Nikkei (Japan), the Kospi (Korea), and the Hang Seng and Shanghai (China) are the more influential Asian-related markets. They open early evening, Eastern Time, and close in the middle of the night. News, and changes in market prices overnight, can have an early influence on U.S. futures markets; read the international headlines first thing every morning.

European markets open about 3:30 a.m., Eastern Time, and close at 11:30 a.m. ET. Those markets, the Euro movement, and the ECB (European Central Bank) are also very influential on U.S. markets.

U.S. e-mini stock index futures markets are open from 6:00 p.m. to 4:15 p.m. daily, ET (22+ hours). Oil stops trading at 2:30 p.m. ET; oil futures continue trading. The greatest e-mini futures activity is usually from about 7:00 a.m. to 11:30 a.m., ET (when the European markets close), and 2:30 p.m. to 4:00 p.m., ET close. Early evening trading of e-mini futures (e.g. 6:00 - 10:00 p.m. ET) is not advised as there are few traders in the market at that time, and volume and volatility are very low. The /EMD is especially thinly traded at that time, and hardly registers on shorter time frames.

Records and Taxes

Begin by trading only one contract of the e-mini of your choice. Write down the date, index you are trading, maybe time of day, and the price. Let's say you bought one contract of the /ES at 9:00 a.m., and sold it at 11:15 a.m. the same day. It might look something like this:

Oct 7, 9am, buy 1 ES @2118.25; sold 1 ES Oct 7, 11:15 am @ 2125.5 NET = + 7.25 pts; + $355.

In the case of the /ES, the price moves by a quarter of a point. This profit was 7.25 points (2125.5 - 2118.25). At $50 a point X 7.25 points, your profit is $362.50, less trading fees. Trading fees are about $7.00 round-trip (buy & sell one contract, or sell and buy back one contract). It is a good idea to stay on the low side of the net return to keep yourself more honest about how much you are making. When trading the /EMD, you may round up to a deduction of $10 for fees, since the lowest tick is .1 point, or $10. Your broker will keep track of all these trades and fees, and provide an income statement at the end of the year.

I have been trading for several years, and see lots of + signs at the end of trades. I estimate my ratio of positive trades to be above 80%. Trading reports will be offered in the chapters about trading models.

The following commentary is for U.S. Federal taxes, and should *not* be construed as tax advice. Forms, laws, and interpretations change. This is what I believe to be currently applicable; you should consult with your tax advisor. Most capital gains from trading e-mini contracts are probably short-term in nature. But, because of the complexities of bookkeeping, rules were established to simplify the recording and taxing of these forms of capital gains.

At the end of the year, your net (of trading fees) capital gains are reported by your broker. For simplicity, let's say your net trading income was $10,000. The nature of this income places you under what is currently described as "1256 Contracts," which includes futures and binary options. This $10,000 income from trading e-mini futures is reported on federal form 6781, called "Gains and Losses From Section 1256 Contracts and Straddles." No matter how long you held each of your trades, your total capital gains (in this case $10,000) are broken down into 40% short-term capital gains ($4,000), and 60% long-term capital gains ($6,000). Depending on your tax bracket, this can result in a fairly reasonable overall tax rate.

Chapter 6

Candlestick Analysis

You haven't lost money if you miss a positive trading situation; you've only lost the opportunity to make more money--Dennis B. Anderson

It was mentioned earlier that most technical indicators describe what the market has been doing, not how investors are behaving at the present time. Candlesticks are the best at describing what investors are currently thinking and feeling, because they show buying and selling behavior as it is happening. Daily candlesticks show investor behavior over a daily time frame; 15-minute candles show investor behavior over a much shorter period of time, and illustrate intraday trading behavior.

We naturally think that movement in market prices tells us about the value of the market. That may be true to some extent, but trader behavior is really telling us what their *perceptions* of the value of the market currently are. Remember the discussion in Chapter 4 about how we use current assessments as forms of predictions about the future? Markets move on perceptions of future stock market value, based on current interpretations.

Trader behavior is therefore based on current information, individually filtered, that leads to expectations about future market behavior. Hence, we see market prices move up and down. Candlesticks are the best method for identifying those changes in investor sentiment.

Markets can only move three directions -- up, down, and sideways. They move up if there are more buyers than sellers, down if there are more sellers than buyers, and sideways if there is general uncertainty and/or consolidation after a sustained move in one direction (the market needs to take a pause and figure out what it wants to do next).

Notice the "personalization" of the market in the previous paragraph. "The market" is, in fact, the manifestation of all people trading the market. As they make their decisions, the market reacts. Individual investors are pulling the market levers. As you become absorbed with the market, candlesticks, and other indicators, you acquire a sense of identification with the market and the traders in it. You tend to sense more how others are thinking and feeling, what their goals are, and how they are making decisions. You can witness this on the buy/sell table as you see the moving buy and sell orders coming and going, and the adjustments traders are making in pricing. The more you can get inside this process, the more effective you will be.

Candlesticks describe the three directions markets can take. They also can indicate when the market appears to be making a change in direction. This is sometimes described as making a pivot, or a change in polarity. If the market has been trending higher, but may be approaching a level of prior resistance, certain candlesticks can tell us that the market might be changing direction, and may be moving lower. In a descending market, candlesticks can also tell us where the market might be finding support, and getting ready to change direction and move higher.

Support and Resistance

We are focused on prior prices of e-mini stock index futures. These indexes (markets) have recent, and not-so-recent price histories. If the index has been fairly range bound, meaning trading within a certain, usually limited price range, eventually it will move higher or lower from that range. The longer an index stays closely in the same price range, the stronger the move away from that range will likely be.

If prices move higher, they may move to an area of prior price highs. This is described as a resistance zone. This means that the index may be fully priced for present conditions, and needs some major reason(s) to move above the prior price high. Resistance may also come in the form of a simple moving average. For example, the price may stop moving higher once it hits a 50-day or

20-day SMA. In Chapter 3, I described how traders tend to follow certain indicators, especially moving averages, and trade off them.

In a falling market, prices move down to a zone where they were previously, and may pause there. Traders are reasoning whether there is cause for prices to move below their prior lows. If not, the market may not move lower from there. This is described as a support zone. As in advancing markets, the same moving averages can serve as a line of support against further declines in index prices.

Sometimes there is a mid-level area of prior resistance. If circumstances become more positive, prices may move through, and above, this resistance area. If that higher move becomes solidified, this prior area of resistance above becomes an area of support below. This establishes a new and higher trading range.

One issue you need to watch for when a declining market makes a turn and starts to move higher: short covering. As a market appears to bottom, short sellers begin to "cover their shorts." That means they are buying back the shares they borrowed (sold short) when the market was higher, so they can lock in their profits. This obviously puts upward pressure on market prices. If this move is supported by improved market conditions and sentiment, it is more likely to be for real, and continue its upward momentum. Otherwise, the uptrend may be temporary due to traders covering their shorts. If you see a candlestick reversal signal connected to this change to upward direction, and see other confirmation, you may choose to buy a long contract. This will be discussed in the next chapter.

When markets have risen to new highs, or a high resistance zone, prices may pull back. In this case, traders may be selling to lock in profits from buying when the market was priced lower. It might be prudent for you to take some profits, but don't short the market until you see clear technical indications that investor sentiment has moved to the negative, or sell side.

Candlesticks are especially useful in identifying changes in market direction. Perhaps the best singular candlestick for this is the "Doji."

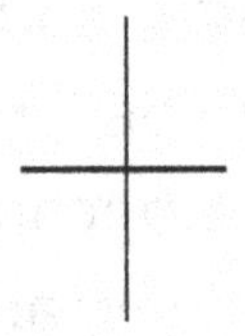

Picture of Doji Candlestick

The main feature of a doji candlestick is that it represents indecision. The body of the candlestick is mostly just a horizontal line, meaning that the opening and closing prices during a selected time frame were identical, or nearly so. The doji can have various lengths of a wick and a tail; greater length of either, or both, illustrates greater indecision. It represents an even battle between the bulls (believe the market will rise) and the bears (believe the market will fall). If a doji occurs at the top of a trend, you should be ready to close long positions, or go short the next day. A doji, at the top of a trend, signals a reversal without needing confirmation. However, if a doji day occurs during a downturn, it needs to be followed by a bullish day for confirmation before you consider buying. In down markets, downward momentum is usually stronger than upward momentum during a rising market. Therefore, there is the need for confirmation at the bottom.

If a doji appears at the bottom of an oversold market, then the price gaps up and opens higher the next day, and finishes positive for that day, that is a very bullish signal. After a long trend, up or down, a doji can also represent consolidation while traders study what to do next. The market may move sideways for a few days, with other dojis appearing. The longer the sideways consolidation continues, the stronger the breakout will likely be, upward or downward. If a trend has moved the market up near its prior high, then several dojis appear, the likelihood is greatest that a forceful downtrend will soon begin.

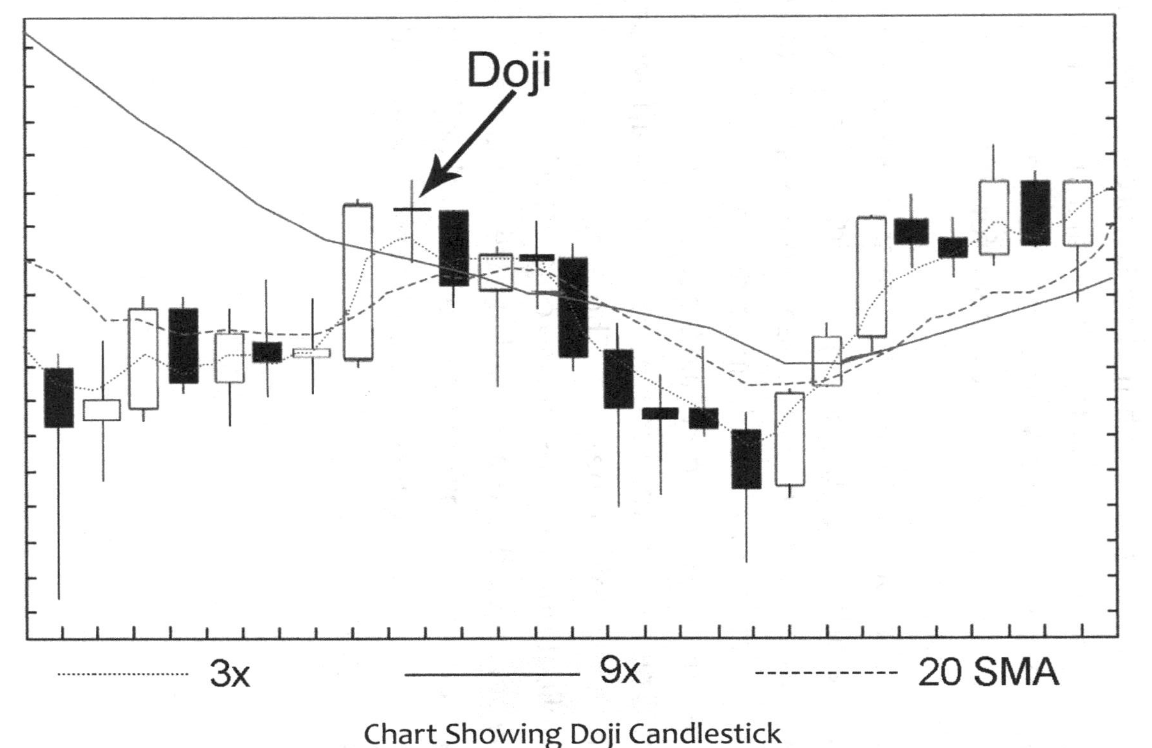

Chart Showing Doji Candlestick

Gravestone Doji

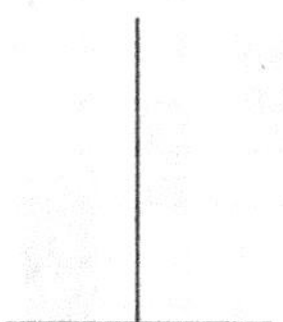

Picture of Gravestone Doji

The gravestone doji is most significant at market tops. The daily open and close are both at the bottom. The long wick shows that the bulls drove the price quite high, but couldn't hold it. The bears stepped in and sold, driving the price back down where it opened that morning. If the price opens lower the next day, you should probably sell immediately.

Spinning Top

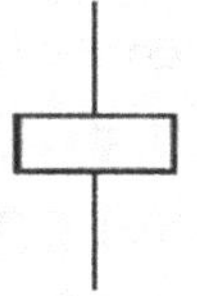

Picture of Spinning Top

The spinning top looks much like a doji, but has a small body. It still represents indecision and the market will likely move in the direction it opens the following day.

Bullish and Bearish Engulfing Candlestick Patterns

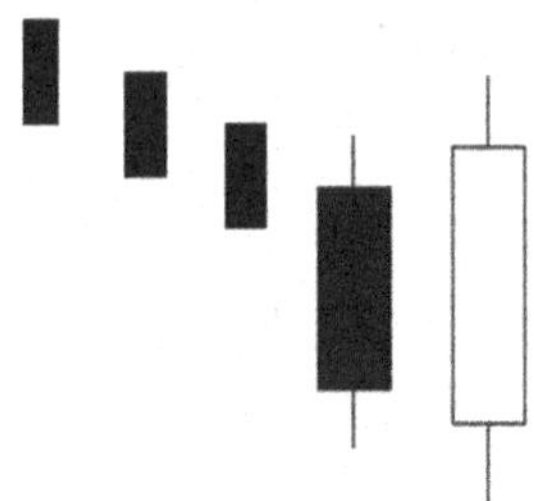

Picture of Bullish Engulfing Candlestick Pattern

The bullish engulfing pattern forms toward the end of a downtrend. In that position, it serves as a probable reversal signal. It consists of two primary candles, one bearish, in line with the current downtrend, and the second one bullish. The bullish candle opens lower than the bearish candle, and closes higher than the top of the bearish candle. Either the open or the close of the second candle can be equal to the bearish candle, but not both. The second candle completely engulfs the bearish candle; wick and tail are not significant. If the bullish engulfing candle body engulfs more than one immediate bearish candle, that is an even stronger indicator of a trend change. If the market opens higher the next day, that is a very positive signal for a long position.

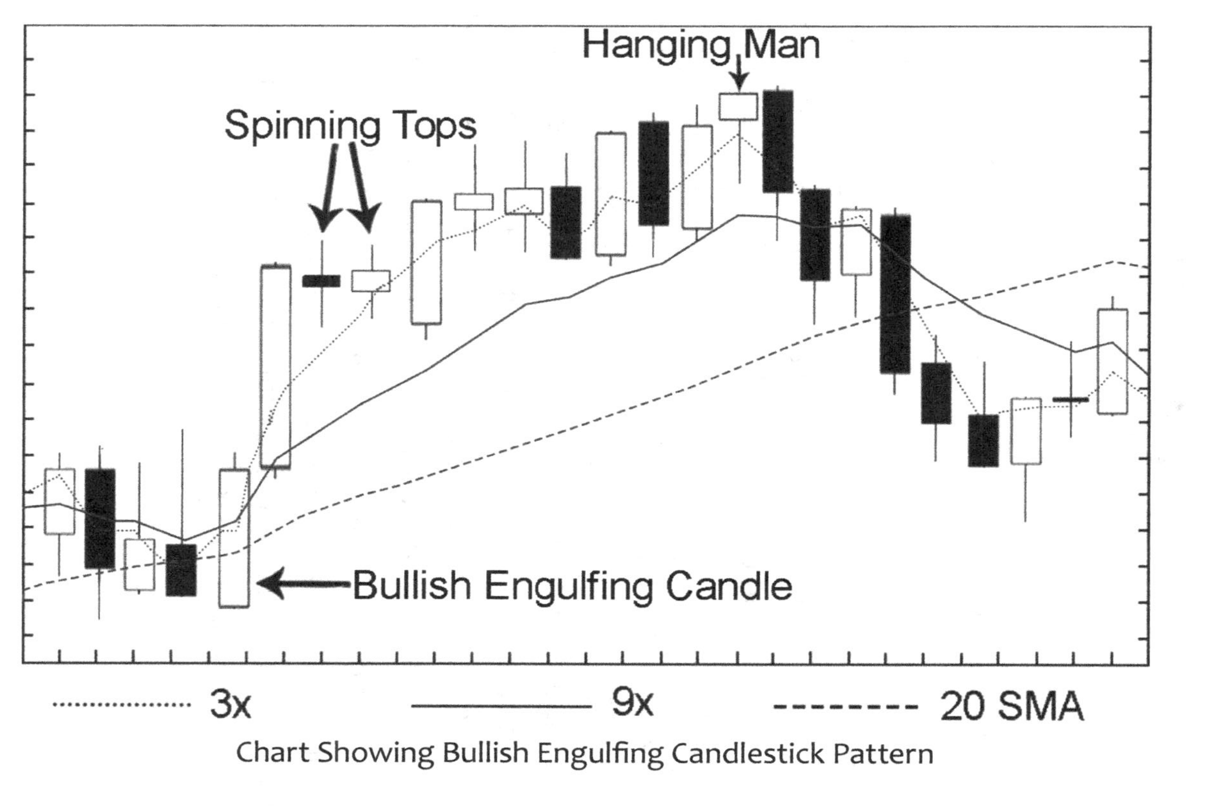

Chart Showing Bullish Engulfing Candlestick Pattern

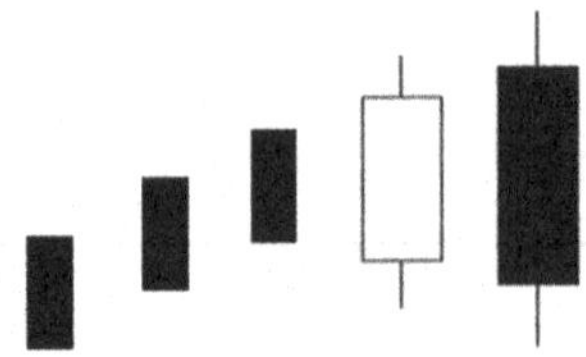

Picture Showing Bearish Engulfing Candlestick Pattern

The bearish engulfing candle is the opposite, and forms near the top of an uptrend. There is a bullish candle, then the engulfing bearish candle opens higher than the bullish candle, but closes lower. Wick and tail are not significant, and either the open or close of the bearish candle can be equal to the prior bullish candle, but not both. In this case, bulls pushed the price above the prior day's close, but the bears stepped in and drove the price down to a point equal to, or lower than the low of the prior day's open. This usually means that most of the bulls have bought, and run out of gas, and now the bears may be taking over. A larger comparative bearish candle at the top is most powerful, and a downtrend from there is likely. If the market opens lower the next day, be prepared to go short a contract.

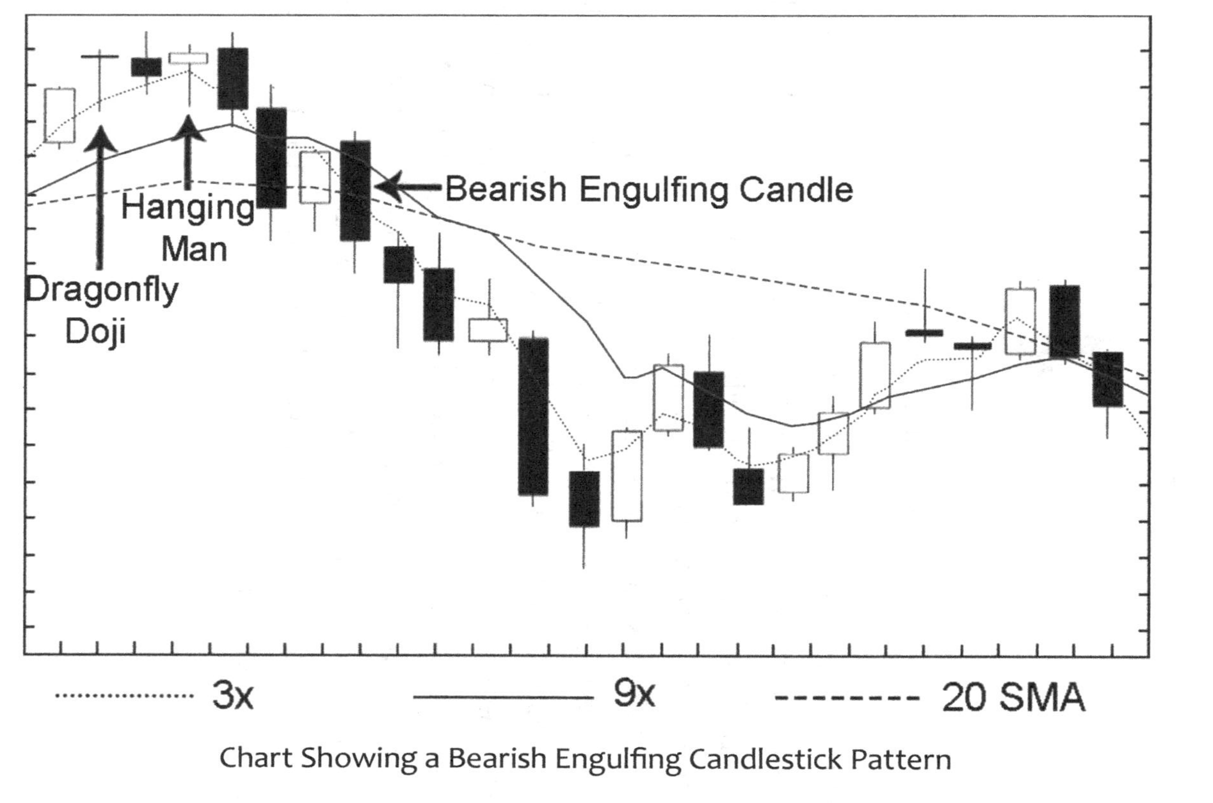

Chart Showing a Bearish Engulfing Candlestick Pattern

Bullish Harami

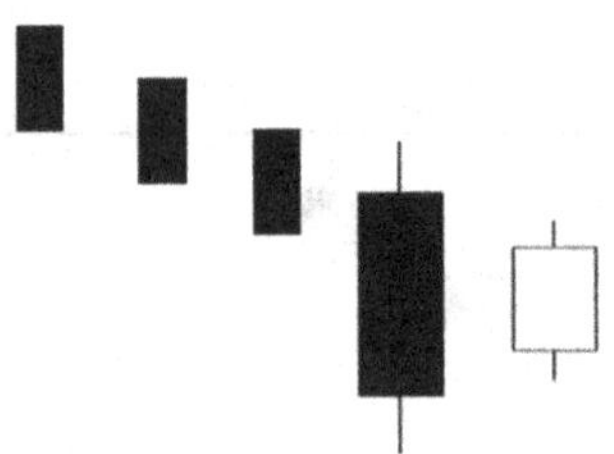

Picture of Bullish Harami

This is a two-candle daily formation that occurs near the bottom of a downtrending market. The first candle will be bearish, consistent with the trend, and should be fairly long. This suggests a final downward push by the bears. The second candle is usually bullish, and opens and closes within the outline of the bearish candle, suggesting that the selling has stopped, and the bulls are stepping in. As in the case of all bearish reversals, this two-candle pattern needs bullish confirmation the third day to add credibility to the notion that a change in market direction is underway. If you get confirmation of a reversal by further upward movement the next day, go long one contract.

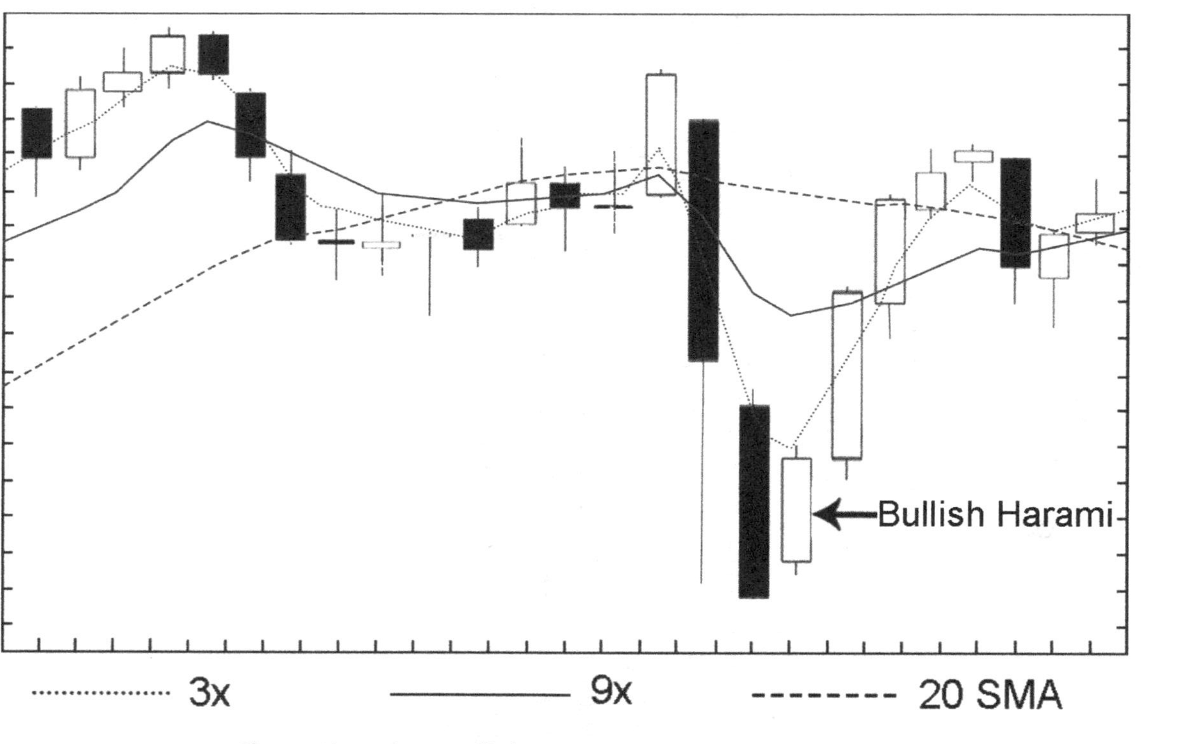

Chart Showing Bullish Harami Candlestick Pattern

Bearish Harami

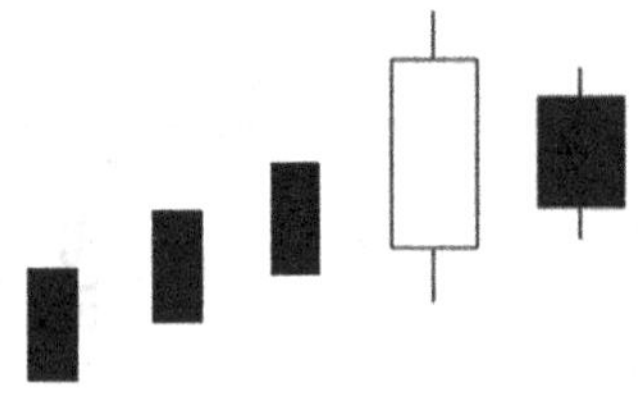

Picture of Bearish Harami

This is the bearish counterpart to the Bullish Harami, and occurs at, or near, the top of an uptrend. It is a two-candle formation, with the first candle being bullish, consistent with the uptrend. The second candle is bearish, and opens and closes inside the body of the last bullish candlestick. Bearish confirmation, such as a lower open the next day, is needed to confirm that a downtrend is underway. If confirmation develops, be ready to go short one contract.

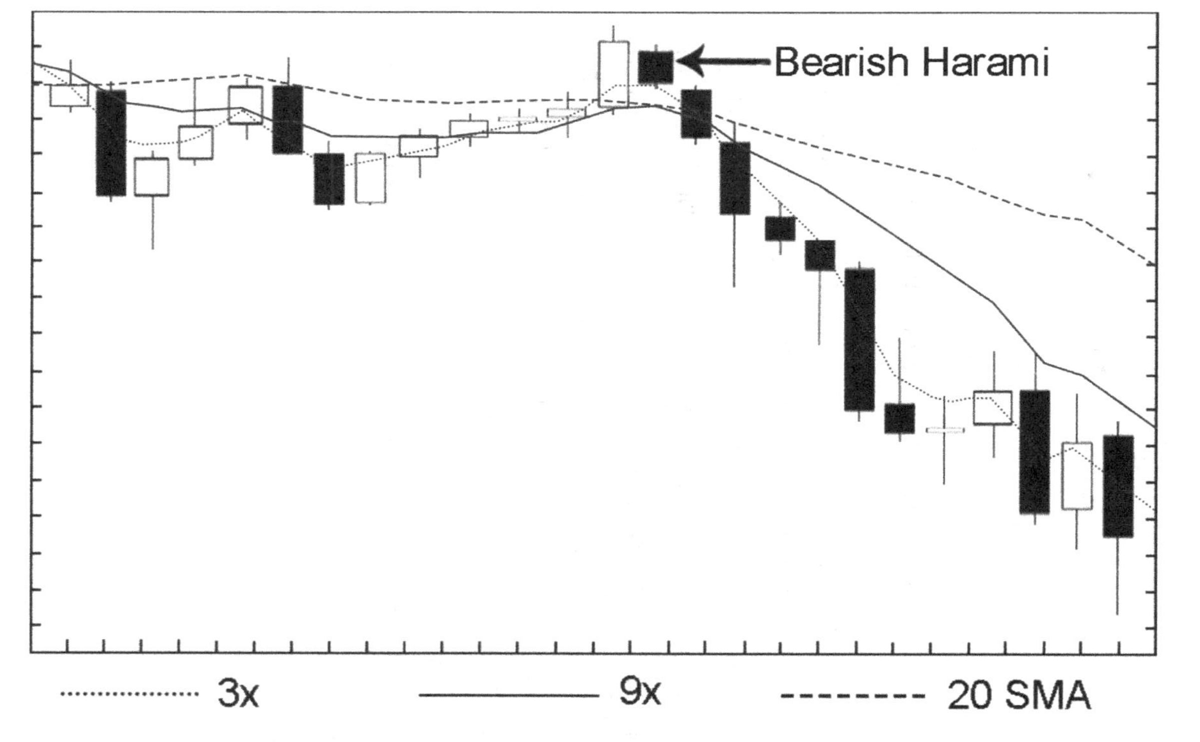

Chart Showing Bearish Harami Candlestick Pattern

Hammer

Picture of Hammer Candlestick Pattern

The hammer appears at the bottom of a trend, and consists of a single candlestick. It has a smaller body, and a tail that is at least two times the length of the body; a longer tail is more bullish. A bullish hammer is somewhat more positive than a bearish hammer. A positive following day is necessary to confirm a likely change in direction. The long tail shows that sellers drove the price down, near the bottom of a trend, then the bulls stepped in and drove the price back up. If the bulls dominate the following day, an uptrend may be in progress.

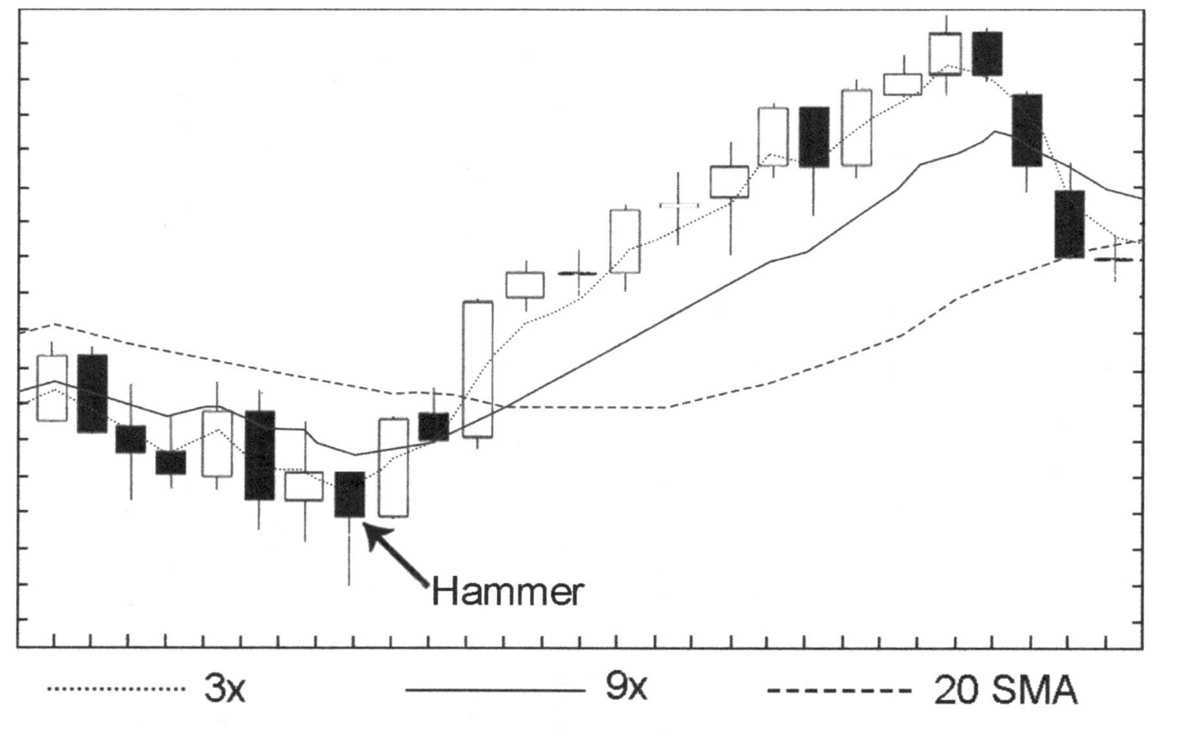

Chart Showing Hammer Candlestick Pattern

Hanging Man

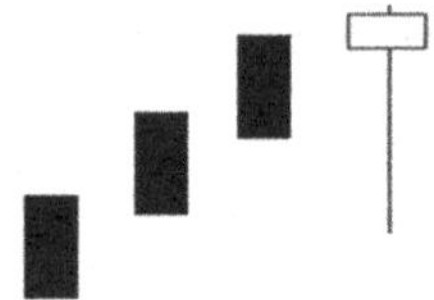

Picture of Hanging Man Candlestick Pattern

The hanging man consists of one candle which looks similar to a hammer, but it appears at the top of an uptrend. It has a smaller body, and a tail that is at least twice the length of the body. There should be no or very little wick on this candle, and a bearish hanging man is more meaningful than a bullish hanging man, since it appears at the top of the current trading range. The hanging man needs confirmation the next day. That day's candlestick should gap down on the open, or close lower than it opened to confirm a likely change in direction. The dynamics are different at the top of a trading range. Buyers are still strong, but the long tail means that the bears drove the price down during the day. If the bulls are now exhausted, the bears will begin to exert their will the following day and drive prices lower.

Piercing Pattern

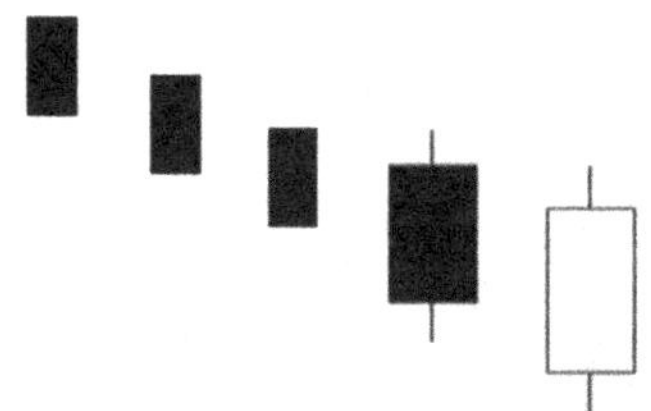

Picture of Piercing Pattern Candlestick Pattern

This is a two-candle formation that occurs near the low in a downtrending market. The first candle is bearish, consistent with the current downtrend. The second candle is bullish, as it opens below the low of the prior day's candle, but closes more than halfway up the prior day's candle, near the high of the day. Though the bears opened the second day's candle lower, the bulls stepped in and began buying, closing near the high of the prior day's bearish candle. The bears are now concerned, and possibly hesitant. If the bulls open higher the next day, and close even higher, an uptrend may be developing. You need the third day's outcome for confirmation that there has been a change in investors' attitude.

Dark Cloud Cover

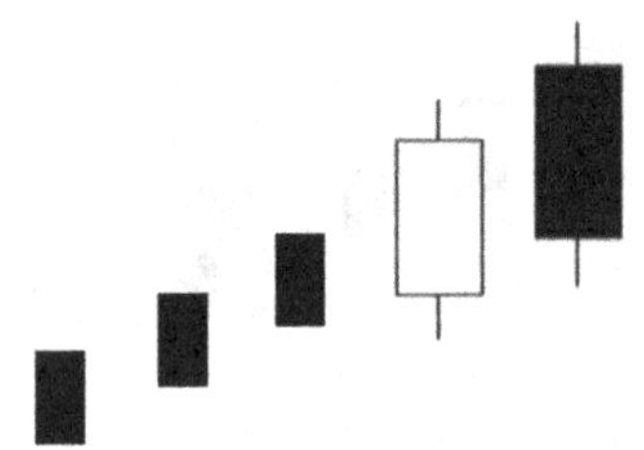

Picture of Dark Cloud Cover Candlestick Pattern

This is the bearish version of the Piercing Pattern. It consists of two main candlesticks and occurs at the top of an upward trend. The first day is a fairly long bullish candle. On the second day, the price opens higher, but becomes a bearish candle, closing at least halfway down the prior bullish candle. The bulls opened the second day higher, but became exhausted, and the bears stepped in, driving the price down. If the market gaps lower on the open of the third day, or closes lower the third day, a downward trend has probably begun. If you see this pattern in process at the top of an uptrend, especially if it is in line with prior highs, you may want to enter a short position.

Bullish and Bearish Kicker Signal Candlesticks

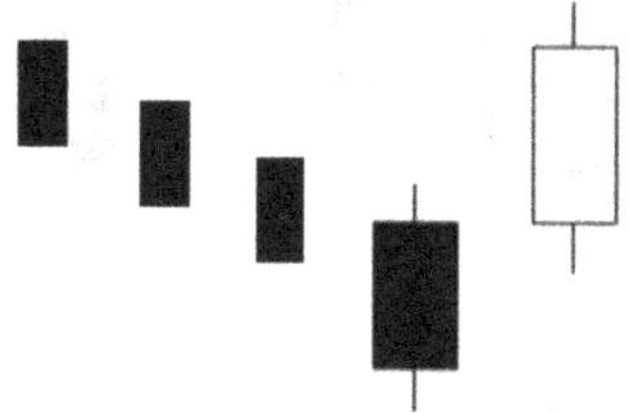

Picture of Bullish Kicker Signal Candlestick Pattern

This pattern is formed by two candlesticks, and is one of the most powerful indicators at the bottom and at the top of trend channels. For the bullish kicker signal, the first candlestick is bearish, consistent with the current downtrend. The second day's candlestick is bullish. The main point is that both candlesticks open at the same price. Since the first candle closed lower, there was a "kick" up on the second day to open close to the same price. If the second day's candle finishes bullish, a change in direction is likely underway. As always, wait for third-day confirmation of this change to an uptrend.

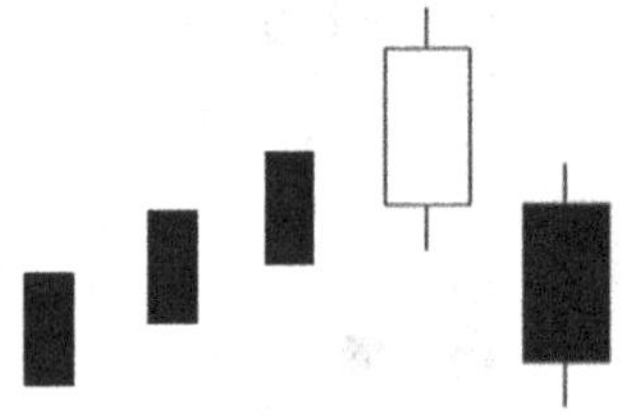

Picture of Bearish Kicker Signal Candlestick Pattern

The bearish kicker signal occurs at the top of an uptrend, and works in the exact opposite direction. A bullish candlestick marks the end of an uptrend, and the second day's bearish candle opens the same as where the bullish candle opened. If the candle of the third day is also bearish, a downtrend has likely begun.

As mentioned earlier, once you have set up your platform, entered the index you want to trade, and set up your candlesticks, then add the slow stochastic chart at the bottom, under the candlestick chart. The stochastic chart indicates the level at which the index currently appears to be undersold or oversold. A level of about twenty or below suggests an oversold condition, while a level above eighty suggests an overbought condition. This chart provides useful confirmation that the candlestick reversal indication is probable.

There is another important indicator to watch for. If the market gaps up or gaps down on the open, there is a good chance of a strong continuation in the direction of the gap. A gap is simply an open space between the prior day's candlestick closing price, and the price at the open the next day.

The following chapter focuses on trending prices of e-mini stock index futures. These candlesticks are extremely useful for alerting the trader to changes in investor sentiment, which often leads to a change in market direction. This usually occurs when a trend channel has become extended. Then, in an uptrend, buyers become exhausted. And, in a downtrend, sellers become exhausted. Thus the title of the first model in the next chapter is "Follow the Money."

Sometimes powerful exogenous forces can produce a quick change in market direction when the market is flat, or in the middle of a range. This could become a reversal only if the pattern change is confirmed the next day or two. If you, and the market, are both uncertain, exit your positions and wait for a clear candlestick signal and supportive follow-up before you enter a new position. In this situation, where the market is uncertain, or choppy, you could trade the second model in Chapter 8, Enjoy Those "Index Bites."

Chapter 7

Model 1 -- Follow the Money

A pessimist sees the difficulty in every opportunity; an optimist sees the opportunity in every difficulty - - Winston Churchill

Model 1 is ideal for markets that are trending, up or down. If the e-mini stock index futures (markets) are moving higher, you buy an e-mini contract in one of the five indexes. If the market is moving lower, you sell (go short) one e-mini contract. (For markets that are "choppy," and not trending, we can use Model 2, explained in the next chapter.)

The first two questions most new traders ask are, "When do I buy?" and "When do I sell?" Fair enough. There are many salespeople out there, especially on the internet, that get you interested by explaining some of what they claim, but you have to join their "club" or "group" and pay hefty monthly fees and/or hundreds of dollars for "special software" to have them tell you what to buy, and when to buy. Most of them deal with individual stocks. Individual stocks usually don't have the upward bias that indexes have, and we all know of Enron and others whose prices went to zero. You also never really know the value of the "advice" you are paying for.

You don't need anyone else to tell you what to do; you can do this yourself. Our focus on e-mini trading with this model is to follow the trend until candlesticks (and other indicators I'll show you) predict that the trend may be over. At that point, you will close your position, and wait to get in again, most likely in the other direction. I'm going to give you a step-by-step guide and explanation as to how you can be a very successful trader. Let's begin.

Get your trading account set up, and be sure you can trade e-mini stock index futures with it. As mentioned earlier, be sure they have a practice account with imaginary money for you to use while you learn how to trade. If you are new to this, take several months to learn how to use the platform, make trades, follow the indicators, and properly manage money.

Set up your platform so it is comfortable and easy to use. Too many new traders get confused, or click the wrong button, and find out they lost several hundred dollars. There are no mulligans. I suggest you have no more than two indexes on your screen at one time, preferably only one when you start. It is less confusing, and you can more clearly read the charts and indicators; clarity and simplicity are key.

You will be using a group of indicators. They work together, offer confirmation of your trading decisions, and several are part of a standard arsenal used by most professional traders. You won't beat these guys and gals, so you might as well do some of what they do, follow the same indicators, and try to get in and out ahead of them, taking your profits and not being greedy.

I wrote earlier about exponential moving averages, those that add influence as their time approaches the end of their period. When you get into your platform, find averages, moving averages, and exponential moving averages; the platform puts one on your index chart. The default is usually eight, nine, or ten as the period. I like to use the nine-period exponential moving average, hereafter known as "9x."

Traders use a number of longer and shorter averages in combination such as 200 and 50, 100 and 50, 50 and 20, 20 and 10, ten and five, and six and three. The goal is to pair a longer-term and a shorter-term time frame to see if they are in sync. If the short one moves away higher from the longer one, or the short one crosses under the longer one, the shorter time period is changing faster than the longer period, and you need to take note.

I prefer to use the three-period exponential moving average, hereafter known as "3x," as the shorter time frame for comparison. So far then, your chart should have candlesticks (probably green and red), the 9x and the 3x. Decide what colors you want these different averages to appear as, then be consistent on all your charts so you aren't misreading important information. The same indicators and colors will transfer from chart to chart automatically. Obviously, all moving averages show as a colored line across your chart, left to right.

Now add a 20-day simple moving average (SMA). Then add a 50-day simple moving average (SMA). Finally, add "Stochastics, slow" under the bottom of your chart. It will appear as a left-to-right rectangle. Use settings of 12, 3, 3. If you have problems setting this up, call or email your platform provider's tech people and they will help you.

The 20-day SMA and the 50-day SMA often serve as areas of resistance and support for many professional traders. And, ascending or descending index prices may find resistance near prior price highs, or support at prior price lows. Simple moving averages often become places where index prices flatten out. An uptrending market may stall at one of those SMA's. If you are at the upper part of the trading range and you get a candlestick reversal signal with reversal support from the 9x and 3x, the fact that this is occurring at one of these SMA's should be looked at as possible confirmation for you to exit a long trade, or enter a short trade.

If you have a short position, falling prices may find support at one of these simple moving averages. As a descending market stalls at a SMA, and you are near the bottom of a trading range, you may get a candlestick reversal signal with reversal support from the 9X and 3X. In that case, you may want to close your short position and consider entering a long position after confirmation.

The main indicator you will follow is the 9x. This describes the past nine periods of trading. That can be nine months, nine days, nine four-hour periods, nine one -hour periods, nine 30-minute periods, or periods of fifteen, five, and one minute. And, most platforms allow you to customize time periods if these aren't enough. If you want to start with more stress-free trading, wait for a trending market with indicators moving with the direction of the candlestick trend, and buy, or short, one contract on a daily time frame.

The specific trading criteria are as follows. Review the candlestick signals in Chapter 6. These are reversal signals, showing a change in trend. Watch the 9x line. In an advancing market, the daily close of each candlestick should be above, or on the 9x, and the 3x should be above the 9x. That means the trend is continuing. There will be days when a candlestick will close below the 9x, but wait for more information and/or confirmation. Candlesticks have to give one of the reversal signals, which usually occur after the market has been trending for awhile, *and* close below the 9x line, *and* the market has to open lower and move lower the next day. If the market has been advancing toward new highs, and stochastics are in the overbought position (eighty and above), that is confirmation to close your long position. Another sell confirmation is if the 3x line has moved under the 9x line in an advancing market. That means the shorter term (3x) is turning down faster than the longer term (9x). And, as mentioned above, this may be happening at the 20-day SMA or 50-day SMA.

If you want further confirmation, move your time frame from daily to a fifteen-minute period. If a change in trend is documented on a fifteen-minute chart, your decision to exit the trade is likely a good one. These indicators work on *all* time frames.

In a declining market, where you have entered a short position, the issues are the same, but on the other side. Candlesticks should be closing below the 9x, and the 3x should be below the 9x. If the market appears to becoming oversold, watch for a candlestick reversal, a close above the 9x, the 3x moving above the 9x, a higher opening and close above the 9x the next day, and the stochastics in the oversold condition of twenty or lower. Also notice if you are at a SMA. This combination indicates you should probably close your position (cover your short).

Trading the 3X and 9X Candlestick Gap

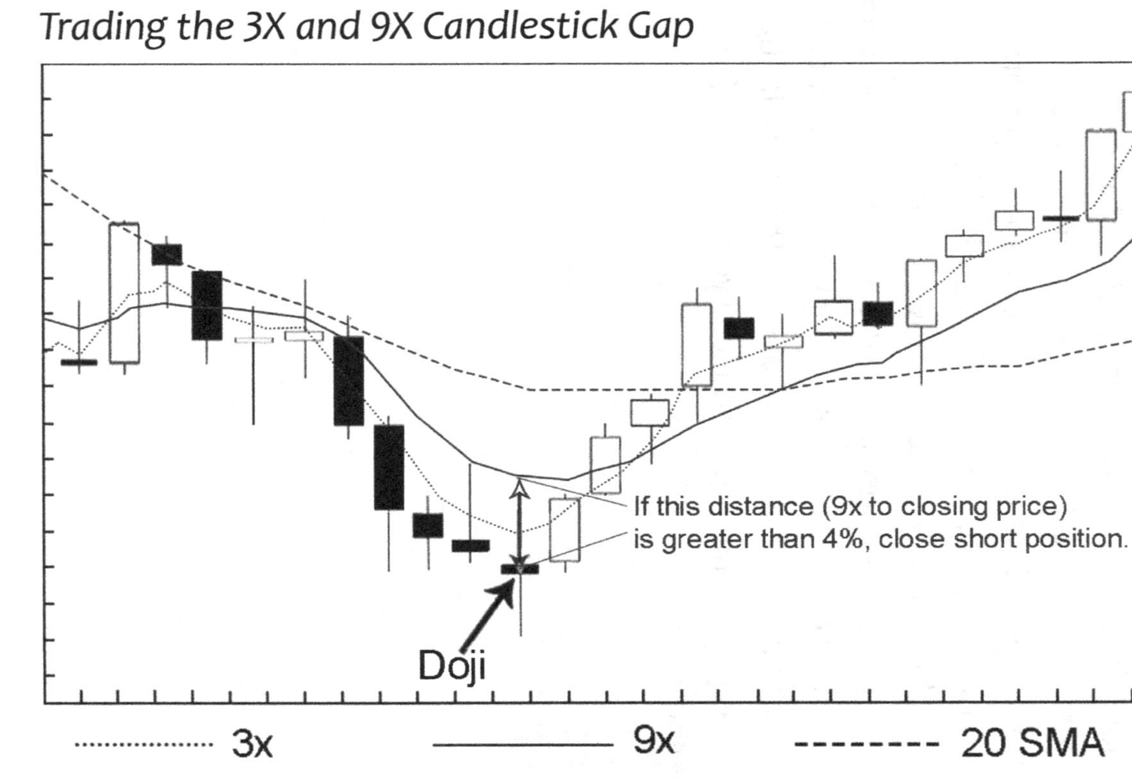

Chart Showing the 3X and 9X Candlestick Gap

Markets usually fall in price much quicker and more significantly than they rise in price. After a sharp and steep decline, the 3x may move far below the 9x, illustrating the exaggerated nature of the decline. If this discrepancy becomes too large, you should cover your short positions at that point, and not wait for a reversal. This preserves more of your profit. That is because a form of reversion to the mean will soon follow, where the index price will recover and move up closer to the 9x. You are alerted to this price discrepancy by the 3x.

In a down market, where you have an active short position working, and the market is close to a support level, close your position when the distance between the 9x line and the closed end of a candlestick body under the 9x exceeds 4% of the price value of that closed candle end. For example, the price of the closed end of a candlestick trading the /ES is 2000. If the price point of the 9x line above is greater than 4% (2080) (2000 X .04 = 80), close your short and take your profits. The price will soon rise closer to the 9x price, probably around 2070. That leaves you with 70 points X $50 a point profit ($3500) by closing earlier. Even if the market continues a bit lower, you will seldom make more money by waiting for a clear reversal signal, especially if your contract price has fallen to prior support levels in the market.

It occurs less often, but the same principle applies in a strongly rising market. When you approach prior market highs, there is sometimes a final, frenetic rush of buyers at the top. Those are traders who have been holding out, waiting for the market to come back down in price so they can buy. But, they decide they can wait no longer, and rush in near the top (they buy high and sell lower).

At the top, the 3x can rise far above the 9x. If a candlestick closing price exceeds four percent of the distance between the 9x line and the close of that higher candle, sell your long position. Price will soon be moving lower toward the 9x. Using the /ES again, let's say the value at the 9x line is now 2200. If the value at the closed end of the candlestick body above is greater than 2288 (4% X 2200 = 88), sell your long position, and take profits. This elevated price above 2288 will likely soon fall to about 2210, or lower. In this scenario, you could have an added profit of about $3900 (78 points @ $50 a point). As this is taking place, there may soon be reversal signals and a chance to short one contract for the way back down.

To learn how to read this package of indicators and practice where you might use entrance and exit points for trading, scroll back at least six months on charts of the /ES, /NQ, and /YM. (I mention these three because they have the highest volume and are widely traded.) Using a daily time period, with all your indicators in place, slowly move forward, find the trends, and write down the dates and prices where you might have entered and exited trades. Sometimes you can hold a trade, such as a long position in an extended uptrend, for weeks at a time. When you see indications of where you should close that trade, you may have made hundreds or perhaps thousands of dollars. Be honest about where you would get in and out, as if you didn't have any idea what was coming next, then calculate your profits. If moving averages are flat (horizontal), volatility is low, and prices are trading in a more narrow range, don't trade this model! In a boring or choppy market, trade the model in chapter 8.

Of course, there will be times when you buy, or go short, only to see the market reverse against you due to something unexpected. If that happens, close the position immediately. You can always take the same position later; better to lose a few points than ride a loser. You will get back in fairly soon.

The indicator package will work well if conditions are expected and routine. It is unexpected economic, and political reports and statements that disrupt the market. These issues were described in Chapter 3. That is why you should review news that developed from other countries over night, and familiarize yourself with reports and events that will come out when you are awake and can monitor your active positions.

Algorithms

It is also important to understand the role of algorithms in trading. An algorithm is a formula or procedure used to solve a problem. In mathematics and computer science, it is a step-by-step set of operations to be performed. It can also include automatic reasoning tasks; this is how algorithms are used in trading.

Programmers set computers to buy or sell investment products based on variables such as price, volume, moving averages, and other indicators. Computers can also read newspapers and reports, and are programmed to initiate trading actions based on key words or phrases. Since they are automated, their trading actions are essentially instantaneous.

After their introduction, it was estimated at one time that about eighty percent of all stocks traded were initiated by algorithms. After more traders started using them, their competitive edge was lessened, and limitations were installed in some quarters. Their use has subsequently diminished somewhat. Nevertheless, their impact is felt in terms of volume and volatility they bring to the market.

The impact of algorithms is especially noticed when negative market-related news is released. Sell programs are immediately initiated. As the price of stocks begins to drop, other algorithms set to less stringent levels are triggered, creating a cascading effect. The market almost always overreacts to these headlines, and that usually presents a trading opportunity as prices will usually recover most of their losses within twenty to forty minutes. Notice the point range of an hourly candlestick during the time a market-moving report or announcement is released; it is usually quite excessive. So, if you expect an exaggerated down move in a previously stable and healthy market, consider buying a contract on the downward spike lower. Set a limit buy order about one-half percent below the price right before the announcement. If it spikes down to your buy price, set a limit sell at the announcement price, or a point or two below the announcement price. I have made several hundred dollars in about one minute using this technique, but don't recommend it, as it is quite risky. Remember, there are no guarantees.

Protective Stops

Most traders use a stop loss to protect against the market turning and moving against them. This minimizes your loss on a long or short trade. This is especially useful if you will not be able to monitor your position on a regular basis. A popular method is to set your stop at the halfway point of the candle prior to the candle you used to initiate your trade.

If I have initiated a long trade, and it is moving briskly in the chosen direction, say at least nine points, I often set the stop at one or two points *above* the buy price. That way, if the market should reverse, I am guaranteed a small profit. Too often, you can get whipsawed when the price backs up, stops you out, then returns to move in the favored direction. Only now, your position is closed out, and you may have recorded a small loss. If you are quick on your feet and conditions are still favorable, re-enter this trade as early as possible for another go.

Also, remember the earlier discussion of trailing stops. If your trade continues in a chosen direction, you can move your stop gradually in the same direction, locking in greater profits as your trade moves along. As you get better at this, you can experiment with whatever approach you are most comfortable with. Above all, do *not* hang on to losing positions. You can always get back in, often at even better prices than where you exited. Trading fees are not expensive, and are not an excuse to hang on and increase your losses.

Model 1, "Follow the Money" Trading Summary

Uptrend. The market has been in a sustained uptrend, and may be approaching prior highs. A candlestick sell signal, or pattern, appears with the price closing below the 9x. The next day the market opens lower, and moves lower. The 3x has moved under the 9x. Other possible confirmations: Stochastics are above eighty, in the overbought position. Prices may have run into resistance at the top by hitting one of the popular moving averages, or getting close to prior highs. Close the trade, and consider shorting.

Downtrend. The market has been in a sustained downtrend, and may be approaching prior lows. A candlestick buy signal, or pattern, appears with the price closing above the 9x. The market opens higher the next day, and closes higher that day. The 3x has moved under and above the 9x. Other possible confirmations: Stochastics are below twenty, in the oversold position. Prices may have run into prior lows, or support at the bottom by hitting one of the popular moving averages. Close your short position, and look to go long.

Keep an eye on the 3x and the discrepancy between current prices and the price value at the 9x. Stay alert for news items that can seriously affect the market and its direction. You may be forced to close your position, depending on world and national political and economic headlines.

What to trade?

The next chapter has detailed information about the five e-mini stock indexes you will be able to trade. You might want to begin with the /YM (DOW) or /ES (S&P 500). They are widely traded, least volatile of the indexes, and put the least capital at risk. You should have at least $10,000 to $15,000 in your account to trade one contract. Just one contract should enable you to net, on average, at least $40,000 in twelve months, trading part-time. As your account grows, you can trade other indexes, or eventually trade in more than one index. Once you get rolling, you can make $100,000 or more each year, trading this model, or Model 2 in the next chapter, on a part-time basis. Model 3, explained in chapter 9, also has the potential to make extraordinary profits whenever the market suffers a severe correction. Each year, leave at least ten percent of profits in your account. As the indexes appreciate in price, margins will be greater, and any losses may be greater due to the increased price value. Stay focused and disciplined, and don't get greedy. Let the money come to you.

Chapter 8

Model 2 -- Enjoy Those "Index Bites"

Those who are unwilling to invest in the future haven't earned one. - - H. W. Lewis

Model 2 involves short-term trading that works in any market environment, and is particularly useful when the market appears to be going nowhere. A sideways market has less volatility, or movement in index prices. Or, it has more volatility, with a greater range of price movement. Traders refer to this kind of market environment as choppy, and don't like it. They prefer markets that are trending, with sustained movement upward, or downward as described in Chapter 7. They also like momentum, which involves a steeper and more energetic trend. For us, however, this type of dull market environment is perfect for picking up steady profits.

For example, during the first six months of 2015, the e-mini stock indexes moved within a fairly narrow range. Historical data is a bit difficult to obtain since the e-minis reset every quarter, and the /EMD is thinly traded. So,

I selected the indexes that the e-minis represent to illustrate this situation.

Index	12/31/2014	Low	High	6/30/2015
DOW	17823	17165	18290	17620
S & P 500	2059	1993	2130	2063
Nasdaq	4736	4570	5154	4987
Russell 2000	1205	1155	1295	1254
Midcap 400	294	256	281	273

To describe a foundation for this model, I need to explain the developmental history. Through the years I learned to trade stocks, index funds, exchange traded and sector funds, and forex (international currencies). Those were interesting, but lacked dynamic possibilities for solid and predictable profits. Eventually, I found my way to the e-mini stock index futures.

In 2010 I began learning about and experimenting with the e-minis described in this book. Part of this process, for me, is what I describe as "absorption." I believe successful trading in this area involves a form of "zen" experience. That is, you have to "get inside" the market, which means to feel what other traders must be feeling, and think the way other traders are thinking. You develop a real feel for the market, its movements, and its changes in direction. You sense how other traders are reacting to information feeds, and how they trade off different information and indicators. You trade off their expected buy/sell reactions and those of their computers. You learn to trade with them and anticipate what they will do. When trading a long position, you learn to get in above the low, but get out below the high where you know selling will begin. The same notions are in play when trading short positions.

I experimented with different models, and practiced them for about one year; it was an interesting challenge. I made a few thousand dollars during the Fall of 2012. Then in 2013 I began trading more seriously, using primarily this "index bites" model, carefully grabbing a few points here and there. Net trading income for 2013 was about $38,000.

I have always approached trading as a part-time challenging hobby. In 2014, now having about $73,000 in my trading account, I became a bit more aggressive in determination and commitment. That year, using mostly the "index bites" methodology, I netted about $143,000.

I was now hooked, and thoroughly enjoying this. In December, 2014, and January, 2015, I moved some investments into a second large trading account for myself, and added two smaller trading accounts for relatives.

We are now back to the first six months of 2015. By now, I was trading several contracts in my two large accounts, and one or two contracts in the two smaller accounts. Using variations of the "index bites" methodology, the total mean average for these four accounts was over $10,300 a week for the first six months of 2015, resulting in profits of about $268,000 for the first half of 2015.

This illustrates that you can make good money when the market is predominately choppy.

How to Set Up the "Index Bites" Model

This trading consists of making semiannual calculations, then grabbing a few index points on a regular basis, thus the name "Index Bites." Trade with a fifteen-minute time frame, moving longer and shorter as needed to evaluate your trade action.

Every six months (choose from about June one, September one, December one, and March one), calculate the daily price range of the candlesticks, including wicks and tails, for each e-mini index you plan to trade, going back thirty trading days, about six weeks of trading. Since prices are reset around mid-March, mid-June, mid-September, and mid-December, the dates mentioned above will allow you to get complete and consistent data since you will be deep into each quarter.

Write down the number of range points in each of the past thirty trading days. For example, if the /ES traded between 2110 and 2130 on a particular day, you would write down "20" for that day. Once you have completed these thirty calculations, rank-order them, high to low. Then write down the range of these thirty numbers, such as 60 and 12, describing the greatest range day and the smallest range day. Next, calculate the mean average of those thirty numbers, and the median (these were explained in Chapter 3). If one or two extreme scores have inflated the mean over the median, reason out a compromise between them.

My research indicates that a reasonable profit goal is to trade for twenty percent of the average daily range on each trade. So, if the average daily range is twenty-five, your profit goal on each trade would be five points (25 points X .20 = 5). This figure also represents about 35% to 45% of the lowest daily range over the past six weeks. In other words, you have a very good chance of being successful with this formula. For the /ES, five points grosses $250. If you trade only one contract of the /ES, and grab five points just six times a week, you gross $1500 that week, or about $75,000 per year.

Of course, if you catch a nice run in price, you can leave the trade in and make extra profits. Or, use a trailing stop. You could make this trade at what could be the bottom of a trend. In that case, you could let it ride, using the guidelines for Model 1, Follow the Money.

You now have a clearer idea about when to sell, but not when to buy. For the "Index Bites" model, let's focus on a sideways or choppy market; Model 1 describes how to trade a trending market. Of course, if you prefer, you could make short-term index bite trades from trending data, using indicators of Model 1.

Sideways markets have a fairly clear trading range, where prices have an upper price range and a lower price range. Take the cursor line for your trading platform, be on a daily chart, and go near the bottom of the current trading range. Then scroll backwards for at least twenty days. Are there any closes lower than current prices? If not, you have a good idea about where the bottom of the range is. Then, do the same for the upper range. Does that appear generally confined as well? Are there moving averages near the top acting as resistance? Are there moving averages near the bottom of this range acting as support?

What are the latest economic and political news headlines? Are traders waiting for minutes from the latest Federal Reserve meeting? Is the chair of the Federal Reserve Committee going to soon speak in front of the House or Senate? When trading a boring market, you welcome benign data and information. Remember, there are two main reasons the market is range bound and choppy: there are enough cautions in the market that traders have little interest in buying and trying to push prices higher. And, the economy and other variables are all right, and getting by, so there is no clear reason to sell off the market. And, as was the case from about 2009 to 2016, the Federal Reserve maintained a zero interest rate policy, providing a floor under the market. Many traders and investors sit on their hands, waiting for something to happen. This is when we can make great profits.

So, be informed as to whether any headlines may be coming out that might roil the market. If none, get ready to trade. (A reminder of the resource for this information mentioned in Chapter 3: http://www.investing.com/economic-calendar/.) The market is often quite volatile the hour before it opens to the hour after it opens. If there are sell orders on the open, and prices dip into the lower range, buy one contract and look to sell after it rises a few points. Sometimes, price will drift a bit lower after you buy, but will soon move up from the lower limits of the range. The same might happen when you short. If there are no headlines that might explain this point move against your trade, let it ride a few points; it usually comes back and gives you a successful trade. My trades have been overwhelmingly positive.

How to Incorporate Trading E-mini Stock Index Futures Into Your Portfolio

Examples require assumptions. Assume someone has a total investment portfolio of $400,000. It earns, or is expected to earn 7% each year. So, the portfolio earns $28,000 that year.

Let's say this person decides to put only 5% ($20,000) of this portfolio into an e-mini trading account. If he/she uses the "Index Bites" model, and only nets $320 each week in this account, she will accrue $16,000 in 50 weeks. That means you only have one or two net successful trades each week, trading only one contract. This is an extremely low expectation. Nevertheless, this $16,000 net profit is a return of 80% on the $20,000 trading account.

This change has a significant influence on your annual return. If 95% of your assets return 7%, that yields $26,600. Add the $16,000 you made trading the 5%, and your total annual return is $42,600, an increase of 52%. That total return is now 10.65% for the year, not 7%.

If you have $200,000 earning 7%, and are willing to dedicate 10% of that amount ($20,000), the profit increase is more significant. The remaining $180,000 at 7% yields $12,600. Add the $16,000 trading profit, and your total income on this $200,000 is now $28,600, a return of 14.3% for the year. That is more than a 100% annual increase in your total investment outcome.

Let's take this a little further. After you study and practice, it would not be surprising if you would make $30,000 the first year on your $20,000 account, an average of only $600 net per week. On a $400,000 account, this would result in an annual return of $56,600, or 14.15%. On a $200,000 account, this would result in a return of $42,600, or 21.3% for the year. Even small trading accounts, carefully managed, can double or dramatically increase your overall annual returns.

Trading a Compressed Range

Volatility in stock index futures is desirable. But, on slow days, money can also be made, taking regular "small bites" throughout the day. It might be useful to review two of those trading days. On Monday, October 26, 2015, trading volume and movement was minimal, and most of the indexes drifted slightly lower.

In my largest account, I trade two contracts on compressed days, since I'm looking for only about two points on the TF and EMD. The other three accounts are secondary, and one contract is usually traded.

The TF futures was traded on this day as well as one trade on the EMD. When trading smaller moves, these indexes are more volatile and most productive from a risk/reward standpoint. There was a spike up and a spike down between 9:30 and 10:15; these were probably algorithmic programmed computer trades. Other than that, the tradable range throughout the day was about 1153.5 to 1160.5, or about seven points. The TF drifted down, up, down, up, down, and moved minimally the last hour.

On this date, the market had moved up days before, then reached resistance levels and had been consolidating for a few days. It looked like support on the TF would be around 1153, and resistance around 1163. Since round-trip trading fees are $7.00 per contract, I try to get 2.1 points, deducting $10 (round figure) for fees. At $100 a point X 2 contracts, a 2.1 point move nets $400.

These are the three trades, bought and sold in my large account on October 26, 2015:

buy 2 TF @ 1157.2, sell 2 TF @ 1159.3 (net = +$400);

buy 2 EMD @1429.2, sell 2 EMD @ 1434.6 (net = +$1060);

buy 2 TF @ 1154.0, sell 2 TF @ 1156.1 (net = + $400).

Net profit from three short-term trades was + $1860.

I also made a total of five short-term trades (all in TF) in my other three accounts on October 26. Trading only one contract, I netted $100, $100, $200, $200, and $100, for a total of $700. So, by trading off and on most of the day, there were eight positive, and no negative trades for a total net profit of $2560 in all four accounts.

FOMC minutes were released on October 28; that created great volatility, and the market ultimately closed significantly higher. I was playing bridge most of that day, and was not able to trade this opportunity. On October 29, 2015, I made seven successful trades (no losers) between 9:30 and 11:30 a.m. Range on the TF was about seven points, and eight points on the EMD. The trades were:

short 1 TF @ 1174.5, close @ 1170.1 (net = + $430);

buy 1 TF @ 1167.5, sell @ 1170.6 (net = + $300);

buy 2 TF @ 1170.1, sell @ 1172.2 (net = + $400);

buy 2 EMD @ 1444.1, sell @ 1446.2 (net = + $400);

buy 2 TF @ 1169.5, sell @ 1171.6 (net = + $400);

buy 1 EMD @ 1442.8, sell @ 1444.9 (net = + $200);

buy 2 TF @ 1169.2, sell @ 1171.3 (net = + $400).

Net trading income over those two hours was + $2530. These are fairly typical daily results, and are especially telling, since the trading range was only seven or eight points in the TF and EMD.

October 27 was a special day that deserves mention. It was a very volatile day (the day before release of the FOMC minutes), and I was ready for it. It was a trading dream: 32-point range on the TF, and 29-point range on the EMD.

I entered fifteen trades, using all four accounts, on the 27th, and closed them that day, or on the 28th. There were no negative trades. Net trading income from October 27 - 28 was $24,400. That resulted in a four-day (three days of actual trading) net profit of $29,490.

The following pages contain descriptions of how each of the thirty day average ranges was calculated. You might choose to use these as templates for your own semi-annual calculations of the e-mini stock index futures you wish to trade.

30 Day Range Calculations for Five E-mini Stock Index Futures

/YM -- DOW

30 day ranges from spring, 2016

442	167	Range = 104 - 442
360	163	Total = 5749
283	163	Mean = 192
253	159	Median = 169
252	148	Use 180 as "average"
252	144	180 X 20% = 36 points
248	143	36 = 35% of lowest
230	139	daily range
221	138	
206	134	
193	129	
187	128	
182	125	
172	113	
171	104	

36 points X $5 per point = $180 per trade

$180 - $7 commission X 6 net positive trades per week = $1,038 per week

$1,038 per week X 50 actual trading weeks = $51,900 each year

/ES -- S&P 500

30 day ranges from spring, 2016

58	20	Range = 14 - 58
44	20	Total = 746
39	20	Mean = 24.9
37	20	Median = 20
33	19	Use 23 as "average"
33	19	23 X 20% = 4.5 points
31	18	4.5 = 32% of lowest
31	18	daily range
30	18	
26	17	
26	17	
25	16	
25	15	
24	14	
22	14	

4.5 points X $50 per point = $225 per trade

$225 - $7 commission X 6 net positive trades per week
= $1,308 per week

$1,308 per week X 50 actual trading weeks
= $65,400 each year

/NQ -- NASDAQ

30 day ranges from spring, 2016

161	57	Range = 31 - 161
116	57	Total = 1920
92	57	Mean = 64
90	53	Median = 58
90	53	Use 60 as "average"
84	52	60 X 20% = 12 points
82	48	12 = 38% of lowest
75	45	daily range
74	45	
70	39	
68	38	
60	36	
60	34	
60	34	
59	31	

12 points X $20 per point = $240 per trade

$240 - $7 commission X 6 net positive trades per week = $1,398 per week

$1,398 per week X 50 actual trading weeks = $69,900 each year

/EMD -- S&P Midcap 400

30 day ranges from spring, 2016

35	18	Range = 10 - 35
33	17	Total = 572
32	17	Mean = 19
29	16	Median = 18
28	16	Use 18 as "average"
24	15	18 X 20% = 3.6
23	15	3.6 = 36% of lowest
22	14	daily range
22	13	
21	13	
19	12	
19	12	
19	11	
18	11	
18	10	

3.6 points X $100 per point = $360 per trade

$360 - $7 commission X 6 net positive trades per week = $2,118 per week

$2,118 per week X 50 actual trading weeks = $105,900

/TF -- Russell 2000

30 day ranges from spring, 2016

38	17	Range = 8 - 38
34	16	Total = 556
30	16	Mean = 18.5
29	15	Median = 17
28	15	Use 18 as "average"
26	14	18 X 20% = 3.6
22	13	3.6 = 45% of lowest
22	13	daily range
20	13	
20	12	
19	12	
18	12	
18	11	
18	10	
17	8	

3.6 points X $50 per point = $180 per trade

$180 - $7 commission X 6 net trades per week
= $1,038 per week

$1,038 per week X 50 actual trading weeks
= $51,900 each year

Chapter 9

Model 3 -- Buy Low, Sell High; Buy Lower, Sell Higher

A budget tells us what we can't afford, but it doesn't keep us from buying it. - - William Feather

This model is for those of you who have excess capital, but want to spend very little time trading. This is also protection against a severe downturn in the market. In fact, if we have a bear market like we did in 2000-2002, or in 2007-2008, you have the opportunity to make several hundred thousand dollars. You need a belief that eventually the market will return to its prior levels or higher, and be willing to absorb "paper losses" in the process (your account shows losses, but that is the case only if you sell; we don't sell until the market returns to its prior price range).

This is a simple premise: you buy only when the market is lower, and buy more when it falls further. We make decisions based on deciles: -10%, -20%, -30%, and -40%. In

Chapter 2, I summarized some of the historical market data: there are 252 trading days each year. On average, there is a five percent correction every fifty trading days, about five per year; a ten percent correction every 161 days, about three every two years; and a twenty percent or more correction every 635 trading days, about one every two and one-half years.

Let's begin with a basic example using the decile guideline. You put $20,000 in a trading account to trade the S&P e-mini stock index futures. You use the highest price of this index over the past three months as your basis. Let's assume its current three-month high is 2200. You set a limit buy at 1980, a 10% decline from 2200. If the market drops 10% to 19% (10% or more, but not as much as 20%) three times the next two years (its average), and returns to 2200, where you sell, you will have earned 10% three times. Trading only one contract, that would provide a return of $33,000 on a $20,000 account (165% return in two years).

A 10% decline @2200 is 220 points. At $50 per point, that totals $11,000. Assuming the price was the same when the other buys were triggered, you would earn $11,000 two more times after the market returned to its prior price range.

Of course, there is no guarantee the market won't go down 20% or more. If it does go down 20% or more, there are plans and calculations to profitably deal with that. You may have to eventually add capital to your account to cover your temporary capital deficit and margin requirements, but the good news is that your profits increase on a larger proportionate basis than your temporary losses.

I'll write a bit more about this, then explain it in chart form. Same premise as above: S&P e-mini is priced at 2200. You buy one contract @ 1980, a 10% decline from 2200. But now, the price goes lower to -20%. You now have an account negative of-$11,000 (1980 - 220 points = 1760 price, from -10% to -20%). You buy a second contract @ 1760. Your average price for 2 contracts is 1870 (1980 + 1760 divided by 2 = mean average of 1870).

Let's say the price drifts down another five percent to -25% (-110 points to 1650). With two contracts, that is $100 per point X another 110 points (five percent) lower, adding another -$11,000 to your temporary paper losses. You are now -$22,000 in arrears, being down 25% from the prior three-month market top. That doesn't happen very often.

But now, what happens when the market goes back up, let's say to 2200? You are down -$22,000 but own two contracts of the S&P e-mini's priced at an average of 1870. You are 550 points below your basis price (2200 - 1650), but you are now worth $100 a point, since you own two contracts. At $100 a point X 550 points, you will earn back $55,000. Subtract $22,000 in temporary paper losses, and you will net about $33,000 on these two contracts, down 25% and back up to where you began.

This is the "bare bones" model. Whenever the market drops 20% or more, I like to add this wrinkle: whenever the market bottoms at -20% or more, and rises five percent from the bottom (lowest price X 1.05), buy two contracts at that level, and put a stop loss about ten points below that buy-in price (ten points for the S&P; adjust for other indexes). If the market turns back down and stops you out, buy two more contracts a second time after it rises three percent from the second low, which could be higher than your initial price; put the same stop in. You're risking the loss of maybe 12-15 points on the stop out and buy back, but will earn about 450 points, or more.

The low was 1650; 1650 X 1.05 = 1732. Two contracts are worth $100 a point. Let's say we don't get stopped out. Thus, the value rises from 1732 to 2200 = 468 points. Now, we add $46,800 (468 points X $100 per point) to our outcome. We now have -$22,000, + $55,000, and +46,800. Subtract $28 trading fees (four contracts @ $7 per contract buy and sell), and you have a net profit of $79,772 on this -25% market drop.

What if you were trading Model 1, Follow the Money? Imagine the additional profits on this bear market if you were short just one contract and caught only 400 of the 550 S&P e-mini downtrend points? You would have to use a different index for one of these methods, since you can't trade against yourself, but you could add about $20,000 to your profits, bringing your net profits to about $100,000 on this -25% bear market.

Let's take this even further. When there is a bear market, all e-mini indexes suffer badly. If there is about a 25% correction or worse, I not only do what is described above, but I look at the lows of the /EMD. When it rises five percent from its lows, I'll buy at least two contracts of the /EMD index, protected by stop losses. For example, a 20% decline (about where I buy) in that index is roughly 250 points. At $200 a point (two contracts) that is an additional $50,000 profit when price returns near prior highs. Now we're potentially up to +$150,000 profit on a -25% bear market. This process gets us up to trading six contracts, but most are bought in the right places, after the market has declined and bottomed out. All trades are securely within the trading models, and your actual downside risks are limited since stop losses are used.

If a serious situation is driving the market down in a rapid and forceful manner, you do not have to buy at -10%. If you expect losses to continue, wait until the market drops to -12% or -14%, then enter your buy order as a "buy stop" order, meaning that when the market comes up to your buy point, one contract will be purchased. If the market continues to fall, move your buy price down, so when the market bottoms and moves back up, you may have bought your first contract at something like -16% rather than -10%. That gives you six more percentage points (maybe $7000) of added profits.

Next are descriptive charts of the five e-minis to provide more detail about this trading model. The charts are sectioned by decile, so you can see calculations at -10%, -25%, -35%, and -45%. The examples go past even-numbered deciles to illustrate returns from declines slightly lower.

When the e-minis decline by a certain percentage, they are leveraged, so the increase in your account balance rises by a greater percentage once the e-minis recover in price. For example, a 25% drop in the /YM could produce a $65,000 profit when it returns to prior price levels. You may have had $30,000 in your trading account. You will have made about $65,000 (four contracts) on a $30,000 account value; that's a return of 215% on a 25% market decline.

Investing Models and Calculations for Five E-mini Stock Index Futures

/YM -- DOW @ 18,000

-10% Buy 1 @ 16,200 Make $9,000 if price rises to 18,000

-10% Buy 1@ 16,200; - $13,500 (16,200 - 13,500 low = 2700); 2700 points X $5 per point

-20% Buy 1 @ 14,400; -$4500 (14,400 - 13,500 low = 900); 900 points X $5 per point

(-25% LOW @ 13,500) = (-$18,000 total temporary reduction)

Two contracts bought = $10 a point X 4500 points (13,500 up to 18,000) = +$45,000

Buy two contracts @ 14,175 (13,500 low X 1.05 = 14,175)

3825 points (14,175 up to 18,000) X $10 (two contracts) a point = +$38,250

SUMMARY: -$18,000; +$45,000; +$38,250.
NET /YM, market down -25% = +$65,250

/YM (Continued)

-10% Buy 1 @ 16,200; -$22,500 (16,200 - 11,700 low = - 4500); 4500 points X $5 per point

-20% Buy 1 @ 14,400; -$13,500 (14,400 - 11,700 low = 2700); 2700 points X $5 per point

-30% Buy 1 @ 12,600; -$4500 (12,600 - 11,700 low = 900); 900 points X $5 per point

(-35% LOW @ 11,700) = (-$40,500 total temporary reduction)

Three contracts bought = $15 a point X 6300 points (11,700 up to 18,000) = $94,500

Buy two contracts @ 12,285 (11,700 low X 1.05 = 12,285)

5715 points (12,285 up to 18,000) X $10 (two contracts) = $57,150

SUMMARY: -$40,000; +$94,500; +$57,150.
NET /YM, market down -35% = +$111,150

/YM (Continued)

-10% Buy 1 @ 16,200; -$31,500 (16,200 - 9900 low = 6300); 6300 points X $5 per point

-20% Buy 1 @ 14,400; -$22,500 (14,400 - 9900 low = 4500); 4500 points X $5 per point

-30% Buy 1 @ 12,600; -$13,500 (12,600 - 9900 low = 2700); 2700 points X $5 per point

-40% Buy 1 @ 10,800; -$ 4500 (10,800 - 9900 low = 900); 900 points X $5 per point

(-45% LOW @ 9900) = (-$72,000 total temporary reduction)

Four contracts bought = $20 a point X 8100 points (9900 up to 18,000) = +$162,000

Buy two contracts @ 10,395 (9900 low X 1.05 = 10,395)

7605 points (10,395 up to 18,000) X $10 (two contracts) = +$76,050

**Buy two contracts @ 10,890 (9900 low X 1.10 = 10,890)

**(Optional to buy two more contracts when index price rises 10% from bottom at this low level.)

7110 points (10,890 up to 18,000) X $10
(two contracts) = $71,110

SUMMARY: $-72,000; +$162,000; +$76,050; +$71,110.
NET /YM, market down -45% = +$237,160

/ES -- S&P 500 @ 2100

-10% Buy 1 @ 1890 Make $10,500 if price rises to 2100

-10% Buy 1 @ 1890; -$15,750 (1890 - 1575 low = 315); 315 points X $50 per point

-20% Buy 1 @ 1680; -$5250 (1680 - 1575 low = 105); 105 points X $50 per point

(-25% LOW @ 1575) = (-$21,000 total temporary reduction)

Two contracts bought = $100 a point X 525 points (1575 up to 2100) = +$52,500

Buy two contracts @ 1650 (1575 X 1.05 = 1650)

450 points (1650 up to 2100) X $100 (two contracts) = $45,000

SUMMARY: -$21,000; +$52,500; +$45,000.
NET /ES, market down -25% = +$76,500

/ES (Continued)

-10% Buy 1 @ 1890; -$26,250 (1890 - 1365 low = 525); 525 points X $50

-20% Buy 1 @ 1680; -$15,750 (1680 - 1365 low = 315); 315 points X $50

-30% Buy 1 @ 1470; -$5250 (1470 - 1365 low = 105); 105 points X $50

(-35% LOW @ 1365) = ($47,250 total temporary reduction)

Three contracts bought = $150 a point X 735 points (1365 - 2100) = $110,250

Buy two contracts @ 1430 (1365 low X 1.05 = 1430)

670 points (1430 up to 2100) X $100 (two contracts) = +$67,000

SUMMARY: -$47,250; +$110,250; +$67,000.
NET /ES, market down -35% = +$130,000

/ES (Continued)

-10% Buy 1 @ 1890; -$36,750 (1890 - 1155 low = 735); 735 points X $50 per point

-20% Buy 1 @ 1680; -$26,250 (1680 - 1155 low = 525); 525 points X $50 per point

-30% Buy 1 @ 1470; -$15,750 (1470 - 1155 low = 315); 315 points X $50 per point

-40% Buy 1 @ 1260; -$5250 (1260 - 1155 low = 105); 105 points X $50 per point

(-45% LOW @ 1155) = (-$84,000 total temporary reduction)

Four contracts bought = $200 a point X 945 points (1155 up to 2100) = +$189,000

Buy two contracts @ 1210 (1155 low X 1.05 = 1210)

890 points (1210 up to 2100) X $100 = +$89,000

**Buy two contracts @ 1270 (1155 low X 1.10 = 1270)

**(Optional to buy two more contracts when index price rises 10% from the bottom at this low level.)

830 points (1270 up to 2100) X $100 (2 contracts) = +$83,000

SUMMARY: -$84,000; +$189,000; +$89,000; +$83,000. NET /ES, market down -45% = +$277,000

/NQ -- Nasdaq @ 4600

-10% Buy 1 @ 4140 Make $9200 if price rises to 4600

-10% Buy 1 @ 4140; -$13,800 (4140 - 3450 low = 690); 690 points X $20 per point

-20% Buy 1 @ 3680; -$4600 (3680 - 3450 low = 230); 230 points X $20 per point

(-25% LOW @ 3450) = (-$18,400 total temporary reduction)

Two contracts bought = $40 a point X 1150 points (3450 up to 4600) = +$46,000

Buy two contracts @ 3620 (3450 low X 1.05 = 3620)

980 points (3620 up to 4600) X $40 (2 contracts) = $39,200

SUMMARY: -$18,400; +$46,000; +$39,200.
NET /NQ, market down -25%, = +$66,800

/NQ (Continued)

-10% Buy 1 @ 4140; -$23,000 (4140 - 2990 low = 1150); 1150 points X $20 per point

-20% Buy 1 @ 3680; -$13,800 (3680 - 2990 low = 690); 690 points X $20 per point

-30% Buy 1 @ 3220; -$4600 (3220 - 2990 low = 230); 230 points X $20 per point

(-35% LOW @ 2990) = (-$41,400 total temporary reduction)

Three contracts bought = $60 a point X 1610 points (2990 - 4600) = +$96,600

Buy two contracts @ 3140 (2990 low X 1.05 = 3140)

1460 points (3140 up to 4600) X $40 (two contracts) = +$58,400

SUMMARY: -$41,400; +$96,600; +$58,400.
NET /NQ, market down -35% = +$113,600

/NQ (Continued)

-10% Buy 1 @ 4140; -$32,200 (4140 - 2530 low = 1610); 1610 points X $20 per point

-20% Buy 1 @ 3680; -$23,000 (3680 - 2530 low = 1150); 1150 points X $20 per point

-30% Buy 1 @ 3220; -$13,800 (3220 - 2530 low = 690); 690 points X $20 per point

-40% Buy 1 @ 2760; -$4600 (2760 - 2530 low = 230); 230 points X $20 per point

(-45% LOW @ 2530) = (-$73,600 total temporary reduction)

Four contracts bought = $80 a point X 2070 points (2530 up to 4600) = +$165,600

Buy two contracts @ 2655 (2530 low X 1.05 = 2655)

1945 points (2655 up to 4600) X $40 = +$77,800

**Buy two contracts @ 2780 (2530 low X 1.10 = 2780)

**Optional to buy two more contracts when index price rises 10% from the bottom at this low level.

1820 points (2780 up to 4600) X $40 (two contracts) = +$72,800

SUMMARY: -$73,600; +$165,600; +$77,800; +$72,800. NET /NQ, market down -45% = +$242,600

/TF -- RUSSELL @ 1200

-10% Buy 1@ 1080 Make $6,000 if price rises to 1200

-10% Buy 1 @ 1080; -$9,000 (1080 - 900 low = 180); 180 points X $50 per point

-20% Buy 1 @ 960; -$3,000 (960 - 900 low = 60); 60 points X $50 per point

(-25% LOW @ 900) = (-$12,000 total temporary reduction)

Two contracts bought = $100 a point X 300 points (900 up to 1200) = +$30,000

Buy two contracts @ 945 (900 X 1.05 = 945)

255 points (945 up to 1200) X $100 (two contracts) = +$25,500

SUMMARY: -$12,000; +$30,000; +$25,500.
NET /TF, market down -25% = +$43,500

/TF (Continued)

-10% Buy 1 @ 1080; -$15,000 (1080 - 780 low = 300); 300 points X $50 per point

-20% Buy 1@ 960; -$9,000 (960 - 780 low = 180 points); 180 points X $50 per point

-30% Buy 1 @ 840; -$3,000 (840 - 780 low = 60 points); 60 points X $50 per point

-35% LOW @ 780) = (-$27,000 total temporary reduction)

Three contracts bought = $150 a point X 420 points (780 up to 1200) = +$63,000

Buy two contracts @ 820 (780 low X 1.05 = 820)

380 points (820 up to 1200) X $100 (two contracts) = +$38,000

SUMMARY: -$27,000; +$63,000; +$38,000.
NET /TF, market down -35% = +$74,000

/TF (Continued)

-10% Buy 1 @ 1080; -$21,000 (1080 - 660 low = 420); 420 points X $50 per point

-20% Buy 1 @ 960; -$15,000 (960 - 660 low = 300); 300 points X $50 per point

-30% Buy 1 @ 840; -$9,000 (840 - 660 low = 180); 180 points X $50 per point

-40% Buy 1 @ 720; -$3,000 (720 - 660 low = 60); 60 points X $50 per point

(-45% LOW @ 660) = (-$48,000 total temporary reduction)

Four contracts bought = $200 a point X 540 points (660 up to 1200) = +$108,000

Buy two contracts @ 690 (660 low X 1.05 = 690)

510 points (660 up to 1200) X $100 (two contracts) = +$51,000

**Buy two contracts @ 725 (660 low X 1.10 = 725)

**(Optional to buy two more contracts when index price rises 10% from the bottom at this low level.)

475 points (725 up to 1200) X \$100 (two contracts) = +\$47,500

SUMMARY: -\$48,000; +\$108,000; +\$51,000; +\$47,500.
NET /TF, market down -45% = +\$158,500

/EMD -- MIDCAP @ 1400

-10% Buy 1 @ 1260 Make $14,000 if price rises to 1400

-10% Buy 1 @ 1260; -$21,000 (1260 - 1050 low = 210); 210 points X $100 per point

-20% Buy 1 @ 1120; -$7,000 (1120 - 1050 low = 70); 70 points X $100 per point

(-25% LOW @ 1050) = (-$28,000 total temporary reduction)

Two contracts bought = $200 a point X 350 points (1050 up to 1400) = +$70,000

Buy two contracts @ 1100 (1050 X 1.05 = 1100)

300 points (1100 up to 1400) X $200 (two contracts) = +$60,000

SUMMARY: -$28,000; +$70,000; +$60,000.
NET /EMD, market down -25% = +$102,000

/EMD (Continued)

-10% Buy 1 @ 1260; -$35,000 (1260 -910 low = 350);
350 points X $100 per point

-20% Buy 1 @ 1120; -$21,000 (1120 -910 low =210);
210 points X $100 per point

-30% Buy 1 @ 980; -$7,000 (980 - 910 low = 70);
70 points X $100 per point

(-35% LOW @ 910) = (-$63,000 total temporary reduction)

Three contracts bought = $300 a point X 490 points (910 low up to 1400) = +$147,000

Buy two contracts @ 955 (910 low X 1.05 = 955)

445 points (955 up to 1400) X $200 (two contracts) = +$89,000

SUMMARY: -$63,000; +$147,000; +$89,000.
NET /EMD, market down -35% = +$173,000

/EMD (Continued)

-10% Buy 1 @ 1260; -$49,000 (1260 - 770 low = 490); 490 points X $100 per point

-20% Buy 1 @ 1120; -$35,000 (1120 - 770 low = 350); 350 points X $100 per point

-30% Buy 1 @ 980; -$21,000 (980 - 770 low = 210); 210 points X $100 per point

-40% Buy 1 @ 840; -$7,000 (840 - 770 low = 70); 70 points X $100 per point

(-45% LOW @ 770) = (-$112,000 total temporary reduction)

Four contracts bought = $400 a point X 630 points (770 up to 1400) = +$252,000

Buy two contracts @ 810 (770 low X 1.05 = 810)

590 points (810 up to 1400) X $200 (two contracts) = +$118,000

**Buy two contracts @ 850 (770 low X 1.10 = 850)

**(Optional to buy two more contracts when index price rises 10% from the bottom at this low level.)

550 points (850 up to 1400) X $200 (two contracts)
= +$110,000

SUMMARY: -$112,000; +$252,000; +$118,000; +$110,000.
NET /EMD, market down -45%, = +$368,000

Anytime examples are used, there have to be some assumptions. Where there are assumptions, there are places where individual discretion may be applied. For example, the prior charts assume you will sell at close to the recent three-month high price upon which your first 10% buy point was calculated. If you get close to that price, but negative news begins to permeate the market, you may want to take profits and sell your positions a little early.

On the other hand, if you approach that recent high number you used as a beginning basis, and the market still has upward momentum, you may want to put a sell stop under the current price or monitor your account fairly closely, and let your positions continue to rise. Your third option is to sell only part of your positions near the top, locking in profits, then let the others ride continued upward momentum.

The S & P 500 Index dropped about 42% in 2003 and 46% in 2007. In the example of a market drop of over 40%, I added to all five indexes the option of buying two more contracts after the market has risen 10% from the bottom. This is in addition to buying two contracts after the market has risen five percent from the bottom. Exceptional profits can be made when the market suffers a severe correction.

Of course, you have other options, such as buying another index after it has bottomed and risen five percent. Or, maybe you feel like buying three contracts after the market has risen five percent from the bottom. Also, remember that you don't have to buy at these specific percentage buy points. If the market is in the midst of a severe and violent decline, wait until it passes the buy points, such as -10% or -20%. You can then trail behind the falling market, eventually buying at a greater percentage decline.

The five percent rise requirement has two purposes. The first is that it provides positive confirmation that the bottom has likely been reached, and upward momentum will likely continue. The second reason is that this five percent rise adds capital to your account by increasing the value of existing long positions you have purchased, allowing you to buy two more contracts without adding more money to your margin account. The use of sell stops here is recommended.

This buying of several additional contracts should be reserved for the times the market corrects at least 35%. If less than that, prices could turn upward for awhile, but the decline is not over, and the market could retreat under your buy point. This is where you might want to use sell stops, and closely monitor your positions.

This model is fairly mathematical, and does not require much time. If the market suffers a severe correction, be sure you have adequate capital in your margin account. Remember though, that you do not need all this money unless the market has dropped to the point where more capital is required from you. A balance of $20,000 to $30,000 will suffice up to about a 25% - 30% correction, depending on the index you plan to trade. These levels of corrections occur every two to three years, by history.

Chapter 10

Putting it All Together

"Luck" - where experience and knowledge come together. - - Michael Schneider

This material about trading e-mini stock index futures is intended to be inclusive and sufficient for you, the reader, to successfully trade this area. More could have been added, such as detailed information about Fibonacci ratios and retracements, or Elliot Wave Theory descriptions, or Bollinger Bands, but that is not necessary for you to succeed in making good profits.

What is necessary is your continued adherence to discipline, good judgment, money management, and the patience to trade effectively. As I wrote earlier, "Let the money come to you." Don't look for the big score. That is gambling, and that is why the majority of day traders fail. Remember, if you are making $200 to $1000 regularly, sometimes several times a day, you will consistently earn thousands of dollars every month, trading only one contract on a part-time basis. What's wrong with that?

Stay true to these models. After you have practiced, then become an effective trader and grown your account, you can always trade more than one index, or more than one contract on the same index. And remember, if you are in a trade, and you get anxious or something doesn't feel right, close your position earlier than you planned, and accept a smaller profit. No one has ever lost money by taking profits.

I have no secondary gain interest in writing this book. That is, I don't have software I want you to buy. I don't have a website and an organization I'd like you to join and pay dues to, and I don't want you to be dependent on someone else to tell you what to do. As I wrote earlier, "You can do this."

If you have additional questions, or need clarification or information about anything related to this book, you will probably find the answers at investopedia.com. Or, use one of the popular search engines. Since most of this book is original material, there is no reference section.

Paper/practice trading is more than learning the platform and being able to make trades in the normal flow of daily activity. It is getting acclimated to the possible loss of money every time you make a trading decision and enter a trade. It is practicing the use of economic and governmental reports, and learning how they affect market reaction and activity. It is being able to identify market and environmental variables, weighing influences, and integrating them as a collective package.

In psychology, "gestalt" refers to an organized whole that is perceived as more than the sum of its parts. To be an effective bridge player, you have to be aware of all bidding, and what was not bid, body language, point counts, conventions, card placement in each hand, and options as to how you will play or defend each hand. There is a form of "integrated aura" you experience at that time.

There is a similar gestalt when analyzing markets and making trading decisions. For example, if the index drops to a level of prior support, don't automatically assume it is time to buy. First analyze and integrate all contributing influences and indicators before making a decision. Traders have an expression about jumping in to buy in a declining market, "Don't try to catch a falling knife."

Sometimes, old adages are not accurate. Examples are, "If bonds go up, stocks go down." "If oil goes down, stocks go down ." Consumer spending is about 70% of the U.S. economy. Logically, cheaper oil means cheaper gas, which means consumers will likely spend more on activities such as shopping or eating out. Recently, however, consumers seem to be more focused on paying off credit card debt and saving what they can for an uncertain economic future. Cheaper oil is a negative for energy-related stocks, but is positive for consumer-related stocks as it reduces costs of production and transportation.

Great Britain Votes to Leave the European Union

On June 23, 2016, Great Britain voted on whether they wanted to stay in or leave the European Union. Pollsters had conveyed the odds were tilted toward staying, so that was the assumption and stock markets were reasonably content since nothing would change. However, poll respondents do not always indicate the truth about how they will ultimately vote.

Election results were moving the predicted direction, but many early returns were from the London area, a region that was strongly in favor of the status quo. I was doing other things, but periodically checked on election progress. About 11:00 p.m. I noticed the vote ratios began changing as results came in from areas outside London. Within an hour moderators began changing their tone, and I thought I'd better check the stock index futures. Sure enough, they were now steadily falling like the proverbial rock.

I quickly entered two /TF short positions, and set buy stops a few points below my buy-in price, guaranteeing about a thousand dollars profit if the situation again reversed, and the market moved higher. It didn't. Voters decided to leave the EU by about a 52% to 48% ratio. Markets continued their decline through Friday, June 24, with the DOW losing over 600 points.

While stock markets hate uncertainty, there was now a greater likelihood the Federal Reserve would not raise interest rates in 2016. This was a positive. Also, Great Britain's exit from the EU would likely be a two-year process, so what would really change in the next few months?

My sense was that computers and emotional traders had again overreacted to this vote. Stocks would likely not decline much beyond the first two-day reaction and might well recover fairly quickly. Four of the five e-minis reached closing lows of four percent to five percent of the difference between the daily closing low and the price at the 9X line above. That discrepancy is very rarely incorrect as an indicator to close a short position. So, I covered my shorts and entered six long positions total in three of my accounts. Those were one /YM, two /TF, and three /ES. Then I went on a previously scheduled vacation in the mountains.

Fortunately, that analysis was correct and the market rose five straight days, recovering nearly all losses from those first two days. Shortly after returning from vacation, I closed all six long positions, and locked in my profits. During the period of June 24 to July 4, I netted about $25,000 simply by monitoring what was happening with the British election. Furthermore, during the first six months of 2016, I earned over $90,000 trading even though I was writing this book during that period, and spent very little time trading futures. When I'm able to trade occasionally without distractions, it's not unusual to make $30,000 a month. I know if I put regular and serious effort into trading these e-mini futures accounts, I could earn hundreds of thousands of dollars each year. It is especially rewarding to take advantage of global disruptions such as the British vote. As I have previously written, with serious practice and discipline, you can do this. REMINDER: The /TF was $100 per point the first 11 months of 2016.

Returning to the trading models, if you are in a long trade with Model 1, Follow the Money, on a daily chart, you may get a candle reversal signal, including a close below the 9X line. The 3X line may cross under the 9X line, and the market may open and move lower the second day. It is usually a good idea to close your position at that point. *But*, this doesn't automatically suggest you should immediately enter a trade in the opposite direction, particularly if the index is trading near the middle of the range between support and resistance.

If the slope of the 9X is flat, or hasn't changed direction, that is another reason for caution. The market could have turned on a reaction to a major news release. After that news is digested, the market could turn again and continue up, in the initial direction you were trading. If that should happen, consider entering another long trade. The same recommendations are appropriate if you are in a short trade. It is important to have trade confirmation and confidence in your trading decisions. And remember, in an indecisive and non-trending market environment, you can always use model 2, Enjoy Those "Index Bites," and pick up some nice regular profits.

This is the pattern for an ideal grouping of different moving averages in a daily time frame. First, add a 200-day SMA. Remember, in a trending market that is healthy, shorter averages should be moving with more energy than longer averages. Therefore, if you are long the market, an ideal pattern would be: the 200-day SMA is on the bottom, and rather flat in appearance. The 50-day SMA is next, then the 20-day SMA. The 9X is next, with a nice upward slope, and last is the 3X with the highest upward slope. A greater angle of slope shows a greater level of momentum, and there should be some degree of upward angle in most of the averages, with the greatest angle in the 9X and 3X.

When you are short the market, lines of the averages are reversed. At the top should be the 200-day SMA, then the 50-day SMA, then the 20-day SMA. Last should be the 9X, then the 3X. Again, the steeper the angle heading down, especially with the 9X and 3X, the stronger is the downward momentum.

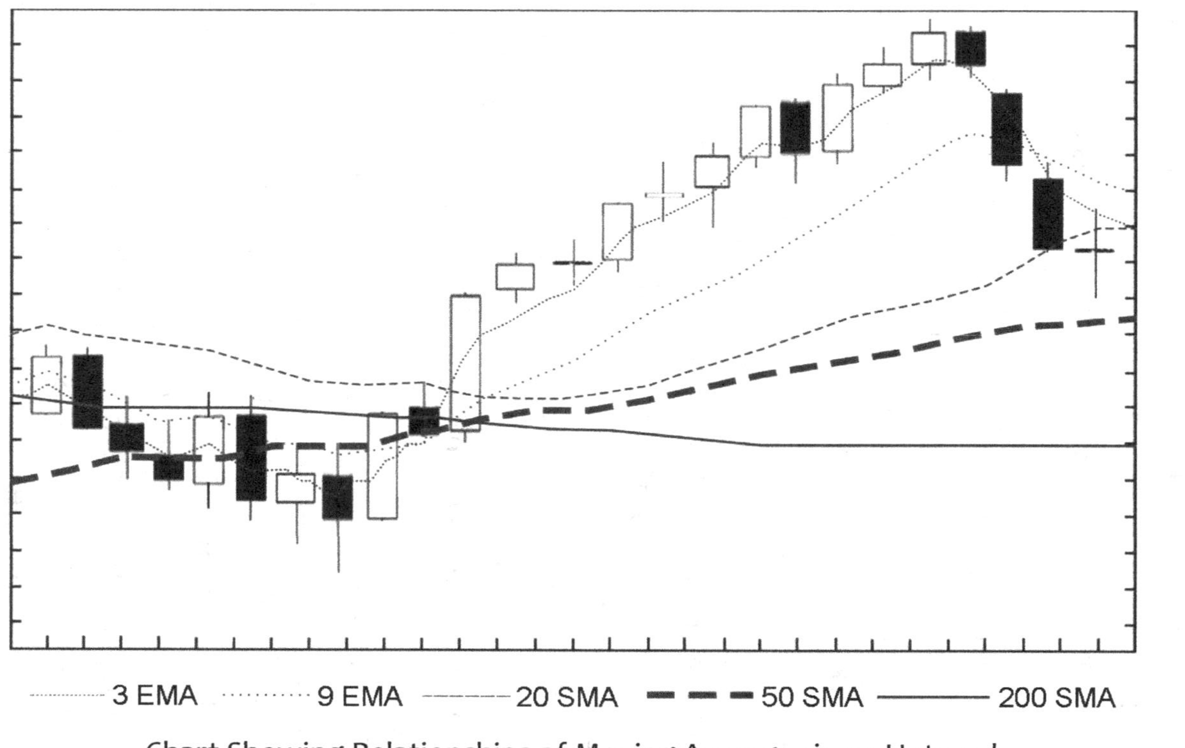

Chart Showing Relationships of Moving Averages in an Uptrend

Earlier, I suggested that you see if the 20-day SMA and/or the 50-day SMA were being viewed by traders as fulfilling the roles of resistance at the upper range, or support at the lower range. In markets that have more recently had severe volatility, that conclusion may be elusive.

Another way to seek more clear possibilities for support and resistance is to look backwards at least several weeks on a daily chart. Search for places where the market has made at least one or two attempts to move higher, but couldn't move past a certain price point range. That could still be the upward limit range for traders. If the current market has moved to that same range, and stalled, and is consolidating, be prepared to close your long position if the price cannot move above those old highs. Then, if the sellers become more aggressive, and you get a candlestick sell signal, and the 3X moves under the 9X, get ready to enter a short position.

The same situation exists if you are short the market. On a daily chart, look back several weeks to see the price range where the market has found support. There should be at least one or two places where prices were taken down, but when they reached a similar price point range buyers stepped in and began bidding up prices. If you are short, and price has moved down to that prior range and stalled, be ready to close your short position. If good news follows, buyers get more aggressive, you have a candle reversal signal with the 3X moving above the 9X, and a candle has closed above the 9X, get ready to buy.

When using Model 3, Buy Low, Sell High; Buy Lower, Sell Higher, you can make nice profits whenever the market falls ten percent or so. Whenever the market is reported as falling ten percent, on average, about every eight months, the mean drop is about twelve percent; this doesn't matter concerning the model, it just reflects a general level of risk.

Using the most recent three-month high as a price basis, you buy when the market declines by ten percent. You can obviously hold the position if it moves back up above the price basis, but we'll assume you sell when it reaches the buy-in price basis. Depending on the index you are trading, you will net between $9,000 and $15,000 when you sell. Let's say you start with a trading account value of $20,000. That means you will earn between 45% ($9,000), and 75% ($15,000) whenever that happens. All you need is to trade one contract and enter two limit-order trades. Total time to manage this trade: a few minutes.

With declines of 25% or more, Model 3 states you should wait until the market rises five percent from the bottom before buying two more contracts. That rule allows some confirmation that the market has stopped dropping, increasing the likelihood that your long positions will begin moving positively. This rule also means your existing positions will appreciate by five percent each, increasing the value in your trading account. That means you will not have to add money to buy these two positions, and it provides additional margin coverage for them.

Model 2, Enjoy Those "Index Bites," is fun and keeps you busy while you have active positions. This approach works anytime, but is especially useful when the market is not trending and has a fairly narrow trading range.

Traders have an expression, "Buy the dips and sell the rips." If the market is reasonably healthy and has some volatility, the expression means to buy when the market dips, or drops a bit. And whenever there is a spurt of enthusiasm, and the market jumps up (rips higher), sell those positions. If it was an especially enthusiastic pop up, you could short for a few points. This is much of what is done trading Model 2.

Trading Lesson

Chapter three discusses the emotional and cognitive brain, and how important it is to learn from experience. Another important point to remember: history is no guide for the future; you can't depend on the past to predict the future, and there is no meaningful basis to say, "It's different this time." *Always remember*: We trade the market according to what it is currently telling us; we *never* trade the market according to what we think the market *should* do, or what we *want* it to do!

No matter how much we study and think about our trading, it is very easy to make ourselves vulnerable to bad decisions. I wrote that I had a very good six months trading a dull market during the first half of 2015. The market had gone nowhere, and I decided to pause and see what was going to happen.

Problems began when I focused too much on market history. This was 2015, and the third year of a presidential cycle. Historically, the DOW and S&P have risen an average of about sixteen percent during the third year of a presidential cycle. More striking, over the past several decades years ending in five had only *one* down year.

There's more. In the past eight decades, there have only been four times when equity markets were up double digits three years in a row (2012-2014 being the fourth time). Each time that happened, the markets were up an average of about 23% the fourth year (2015 being the fourth year).

What is a person to think? That is a lot of historically positive data. I let myself believe in that more than I believed in what the market was telling me. So, after the market moved down some in August and paused, I bought, fully believing that the market was bound to rise. It didn't. After the market fell more, I took my losses and got out.

Now I decided to wait, but hadn't given up on the idea that the market "should" still go up for the year. After all, the main reason for the August decline was just a reaction to China lowering the value of their Yuan currency. And, we still had zero Fed interest rates.

As we moved into December, conditions were looking better. We were approaching the usual "Santa Clause

Rally" period, December is almost always an up month, and we were still lower for the year. Surely, something good was over the horizon, right? So, I bought again, anticipating a December run-up in price.

Unfortunately, prices started down in December, and I had to get out again. So, I returned to the trading models, and earned back my losses. Lesson learned.

That experience tightened my resolve to never let success and history contaminate my thinking and objectivity, and is why I emphasize awareness, discipline, and adherence to these models. Don't get "slick" and think you can game the system. Watch your charts and pay attention to what the traders, news, and markets are telling you.

I appreciate your interest in this material, and hope you will enjoy your new path to wealth!

Glossary

active (open) position Anytime you buy, or go short one or more contracts, your position will move with price movements of the index. Until you close that position, it will be described as "open."

algorithm A self-contained set of operations or reasoning tasks to be performed.

bearish engulfing candlestick pattern Toward the top of a trend there is a bullish candlestick, then a larger bearish candlestick that is both higher and lower than the bullish candlestick. One end may be the same level as the bullish candlestick, but not both ends.

bearish harami candlestick pattern A two-candle pattern near the top of an uptrend. First candle is bullish. The second candle is bearish, and opens and closes inside the body of the bullish candle. Confirmation of a downward change in direction is required before entering a short position.

bullish engulfing candlestick pattern This forms near the end of a downtrend. It consists of a bearish candle followed by a bullish candle that is both higher and lower than the bearish candle. One end may be the same level as the bearish candlestick, but not both ends.

bullish harami candlestick pattern A two-candle formation that occurs near the bottom of a downtrend. The first candle will be bearish and should be fairly long. The second candle is bullish and opens and closes inside the body of the first candle. This needs confirmation of a trend change the next day before entering a long position.

candlesticks (candles) A green or white candlestick shows where the price opened and where it closed higher. A red or black candlestick shows where the price opened and where it closed lower. A wick at the top, and a tail at the bottom show the high and low prices for that candlestick time period.

cerebral cortex This is the cognitive part of the brain which controls all motor functions, learning, reasoning and perception.

change in polarity A phrase that describes a change in market direction.

confirmation When a market move or indicator is substantiated by another indicator.

cognitive thinking This is the thinking and information-processing aspect of the brain that analyzes facts.

congestion area Trading activity where prices stay in an observable range for an extended period of time.

consolidation Trading in a congested area where the price stays in a narrow range. The prior trend will often continue after this consolidation period.

correction This describes a directional move in the markets, usually down in price. Some reserve this term for a decline of at least ten percent.

defense mechanism There are many of these. They describe automatic personal responses to situations we find problematic and want to ignore or avoid.

dogi candlestick This describes trader indecision. The market opens and closes near the same price. The dogi often leads to a change in market direction when it occurs near the top or bottom of a trend.

downtrend Prices trading lower, usually as lower lows and lower highs.

EMA This stands for exponential moving average, a calculation where greater emphasis is given to scores as you reach the end of the selected time period.

EMD This is the symbol for the e-mini S&P 400 Midcap Stock Index.

E-mini The e-mini is an electronically traded futures contract that trades at a fraction of the price of a regular futures contract. This makes it an attractive trading vehicle for individual investors.

emotional thinking This type of thinking originates in the limbic system and is highly interconnected with the brain's pleasure center. When people lose cognitive control they respond impulsively and emotionally.

ES This is the symbol for the e-mini S&P 500 Stock Index.

ETF Exchange Traded Fund is a collection of stocks or securities that has a special focus and trades like a stock.

FOMC Federal Open Market Committee, also known as the Federal Reserve Board.

fundamental analysis This is the attempt to determine the intrinsic value of a security.

GTC This is the abbreviation for a good till cancelled order. It stays active until it is filled or you cancel or modify it.

hammer candlestick pattern The hammer appears at the bottom of a trend and consists of a single candle. A bullish candle is better than a bearish candle. It has a smaller body and a tail that is at least twice the length of the body. A positive following day is required for a change in market direction.

hanging man candlestick pattern This is one candle similar to a hammer, but appears at the top of an uptrend. It should have very little wick, and a bearish candle is best. Confirmation is required the next day to indicate a change in trend.

instrument of application When humans acquire information, process it internally, then select how they will apply that knowledge through their own decisions, they become the instrument of application of that information.

instrument of trading application As humans acquire information about trading, then process it internally and make decisions as to how they will trade, they become the instrument of trading application.

intraday Trading periods that begin and end within the same day.

leverage The use of borrowed money to increase production volume.

limbic system See "emotional thinking."

limit order This is the process of entering a buy or sell order at a specific price. The order will be executed only if that price is met.

linear scaling A scale where differences between numerical numbers are always equal.

long order, long trade, going long the market This describes buying a security with the goal of it rising in price so you can sell it at a higher price and make a profit.

making a pivot This describes a change in market direction.

margin This is money you put in your account in combination with the credit your broker provides for you. This allows you to trade with more money than you actually have, so you have the opportunity to make greater profits.

market order If you enter an order and don't specify a price for execution, your order will be filled at the first opportunity, whatever the price.

mean An arithmetic average determined by adding all the scores in a group, then dividing by the number in that group. A measure of central tendency.

median In a group of scores, rank order them highest to lowest. The middle score in that order is the median. A measure of central tendency.

mode Rank order a group of scores, highest to lowest. Then determine the score that appears most often. This is the mode. A measure of central tendency.

momentum Describes the velocity of a price move. A comparison is made of closing prices over a specific time period.

NQ This is the e-mini symbol for the Nasdaq 100 Stock Index.

9X The 9X is a nine-period exponential moving average used as a core indicator in the Follow the Money Model.

overbought When oscillators or other indicators show that the market has moved upward too far too fast, the market condition may be described as overbought. Buyers may be exhausted.

oversold This is the opposite of overbought. The market is described as moving too low too fast, becoming oversold. Sellers may be exhausted.

paper loss When your account is worth less than before your last trade, you have a loss, but it is so far only a paper loss because you haven't liquidated your position. Price may move in your favor and your loss may turn into a profit.

practice account/paper account An account using real-life conditions to practice trading with imaginary funds.

resistance Selling keeps prices from rising higher. The market may be at or near prior highs, and a simple moving average may be a resistance indicator for traders to sell.

selloff The downward movement in prices due to many more sellers than buyers.

short order, short trade, shorting the market Selling contracts hoping the market will drop in value so you can buy back your contracts at a lower price, making a profit on the difference.

SMA Simple moving average over a specified time period. Many traders follow 20-day, 50-day, and 200-day SMA's, using these averages as possible support and resistance indicators.

spinning top This is a single candlestick indicator much like the dogi, but it has a thicker body. Like the dogi, the spinning top is often an indicator of a market reversal when prices are high, or when they are low.

stochastic oscillator This measures the relative position of closing prices over a specified period of time. There is a fast and a slow stochastic. This is a useful confirmation indicator of oversold or overbought market conditions.

stop loss This is a protective order placed to limit possible losses should market direction turn against you.

support The level or zone where buyers step in and hold prices within that zone, keeping the price from falling lower.

technical analysis Methods of evaluating securities based on their market activity and data generated by that activity.

TF This is the e-mini symbol for the Russell 2000 Small Cap Index.

3X Symbol for "three exponential average," a major indicator in the Follow the Money model.

tick A tick size is the smallest part of an e-mini index that can be traded.

trading platform This is provided by a brokerage service and allows for trading e-mini indexes over the internet.

trading range A zone where prices are temporarily contained by an upper level of resistance and a lower level of support.

trailing stop An order to close a long or short position a certain number of ticks, or points, below an advancing position, or above a dropping short position.

trend A price's prevalent directional movement, up or down.

uptrend Prices that are currently moving higher.

VIX A volatility index known as the world's barometer for market volatility.

volatility The current or expected range of market price fluctuations.

YM This is the e-mini symbol for the DOW 30 Stock Index.

Printed in the United States
By Bookmasters